AMERICAN MANIFESTO

Robin Fawsett

iUniverse, Inc.
Bloomington

American Manifesto

iUniverse books may be ordered through booksellers or by contacting:

iUniverse
1663 Liberty Drive
Bloomington, IN 47403
www.iuniverse.com
1-800-Authors (1-800-288-4677)

ISBN: 978-1-4620-6241-6 (sc)
ISBN: 978-1-4620-6239-3 (hc)
ISBN: 978-1-4620-6240-9 (e)

Printed in the United States of America

iUniverse rev. date: 12/2/2011

To Edith

You're the meaning in my life
You're the inspiration

You're the Inspiration

Written by Peter Cetera and David Foster,
recorded by Chicago (1984).

Contents

CHAPTER 1. The Problem, the Struggle, and the Solution . . 1

CHAPTER 2. Micawber's Advice on Financial Responsibility 12

CHAPTER 3. Human Character and American Federal Lawmakers: The Solution Explained . . . 18

CHAPTER 4. The American Left: its Control over Politicians . 34

CHAPTER 5. A Free-Market Economy, or an American Brand of Socialism? 43

CHAPTER 6. Relations between Nations are Not about Friendship 58

CHAPTER 7. The Iraq War, Pandering Politicians, and Our Safety 71

CHAPTER 8. Iran: Looming Disaster 85

CHAPTER 9. The Labor Unions 90

CHAPTER 10. The Environment, the Environmentalists, and the Politicians 100

CHAPTER 11. The Plaintiffs' Trial Lawyers 108

CHAPTER 12. Federal Taxation, Fair and Unfair 114

CHAPTER 13. What Health Care Crisis? 121

CHAPTER 14. Social Security 128

CHAPTER 15. Pressure from Both Sides. 133

CHAPTER 16. The Only Solution 137

CHAPTER 1

The Problem, the Struggle, and the Solution

American Manifesto identifies and explains what I consider the most dangerous and destructive problem faced by the United States of America and its people. This problem has caused a decline in the economic strength, the international standing, the military effectiveness, and the national character of the greatest nation ever to exist. The problem has brought our country uncomfortably close to potential economic collapse as the result of grossly excessive federal spending and borrowing of money. The problem, to which I propose the solution, is the self-serving, self-promoting, and self-perpetuating behavior of our elected federal legislators, the United States senators and the members of the House of Representatives.

Unlike in Revolutionary War times—when national and personal survival were at stake and federal legislators had compelling reasons to act in the best interests of the new nation—too many of today's senators and representatives act like guests who don't know when to go home. They presume their hosts' hospitality as an obligation and view their hosts' money and other property as their own. They vote and otherwise act to advance their own interests, to the exclusion of and to the detriment of our interests and those of our nation.

American Manifesto explains how and why that selfish and abusive behavior takes place and examines its consequences. This writing proposes the way to end it, which will require our elected lawmakers to legislate in the best interests of the United States of America, instead of in ways designed to serve their own interests. *The solution is to remove reelection entirely from the senatorial and congressional picture.* The only way to accomplish that is to limit federal lawmakers in both houses of Congress to a single term of, say, four years, to be served in only one of the two federal legislative bodies.

While arrogant and selfish conduct of federal lawmakers has been with us since the birth of our nation, it has reached extreme levels. The Constitution established the Senate and House of Representatives to serve us, not to rule us, but that important distinction is not being observed by senators and representatives. Too many members of the Senate and House see themselves as ruling elites and wish to maintain that status.

Federal legislative misfeasance and malfeasance have become intolerable and require correction, partly because many federal lawmakers act like rulers instead of public servants, but also because of a titanic and nation-defining internal conflict that has our country at its most important crossroads since the Civil War. Throughout history bad things have happened to nations when the personal interests of their leaders have taken precedence over the national interest. The selfish conduct of our federal lawmakers, in combination with the internal struggle in which we are engaged, may mean disaster for the United States. The internal conflict, like the American Civil War, has been developing for decades. Unlike that war, this struggle is not an armed conflict. However, its outcome, like that of the Civil War, will have a profound and lasting effect on the strength, prosperity, and character of our nation.

The first important phase of the struggle was the New Deal, which was a product of the Great Depression and federal legislators who favored increased state control of private business activity as the antidote to the economic woes of the time. They determined that the federal government should manipulate the American economy and the behavior of Americans by taxation, spending, and regulation of private industry. The New Deal and the social legislation enacted during the 1930s, affirmed by federal courts that treated the Constitution like a used rubber band, were an unprecedented expansion of the federal government's power as it dictated the behavior of private citizens and businesses. The New Deal was popular with those who, directly or indirectly, received money taxed from others, and it was bitterly criticized by those who did the paying. Politicians in both major parties learned from the New Deal experience that the votes they needed to keep them in power could be bought with other peoples' money. That has been proven to be a hard lesson to unlearn.

As the Great Depression dissolved into World War II, a crisis that deprived America of the chance to determine whether government control of the economy was beneficial or detrimental, another aspect of the growing division became manifest. It had to do with loyalty and national security. It grew out of the war and the rise of the Soviet Union as an aggressive world power. On one side of the struggle were some high-level federal employees who, both during and after World War II, were Soviet sympathizers and, in some cases, outright Soviet agents. On the other side were senators, congressmen, and FBI agents who tried to expose the sympathizers. It was unclear whose side the various government officials who protected and defended the sympathizers were on.

The conflict intensified in the 1960s, to the accompaniment of expanding non-military government spending, defeatism, illegal drug use, and unprecedented unwed parenthood funded by the government. The Watergate affair, which demolished a president and weakened the presidency, was an opportunity that became a victory for one side. The general election in November 2008, with the ascendancy of President Barack Hussein Obama and far-left leaders of both houses of Congress, was a major victory for that side and a devastating, but possibly instructive, blow to the other.

The struggle is between ideas, ideologies, and opinions, but tangible things of immeasurable value are at stake, including our material and financial well-being and our continued status as a free people. I believe a sweeping outcome is inevitable and not far off, and it will determine whether we in the United States of America will continue to experience life as we know it.

Despite the importance of that outcome, and without regard to my own opinions, this book is not written to praise or condemn either side in the conflict, or to advocate any particular outcome. There is an abundance of such writings. Instead, this book deals with how the legislative decisions that will determine that outcome will be made, what sorts of persons will make them, and the conditions under which they will be made. In my opinion, the one-term limit is the only way to negate the self-interest of the federal lawmakers as they make those vital decisions. I suspect my proposal will be denounced by virtually all United States senators and members of the House of Representatives.

Two opposing forces are exerting relentless pressure on our self-interested federal politicians. One side, well-organized and, recently, well-funded, is the American Left. As I see the American Left, it blames America for many of the world's troubles; urges pacifism and appeasement of America's enemies; dismisses capitalism; considers the profit motive (of others) evil; promotes government control of the American economy by means of taxation, regulation, and outright takeover; denigrates Christianity and Christians; and is tolerant of societal and cultural decay. It foments class envy and wealth envy and favors legislation that rewards non-achievement and failure with wealth taken from achievers. Its goals include the expansion of a class of Americans who value government action for their benefit over their own personal accomplishments. It believes that the federal government should have increased power and control over the business activities and private affairs of American citizens. Its goals do not include continuing America's status as the world's most powerful nation. Its supporters include labor unions, wealthy trial lawyers, the great majority of television networks and newspapers, environmentalists, and tens of millions of Americans who see themselves as dependent on government for their well-being.

The other side is not well organized. It is beset by debilitating internal conflict, including recent bitter election contests between the established Republican Party and what is collectively called the Tea Party. The Tea Party, in my opinion, is as much a state of mind as an organized entity. I see this other side as consisting of those who openly love America; who want it to remain the strongest nation in the world; who do not covet money and benefits taxed from others; who believe in self-reliance; and who believe in the Christian God. They believe in minimal government control over business and personal activities, thus favoring increased personal freedom over increased government caretaking. Most of them are not focused on what the Left is trying to take from them and do to America.

In short, the Left has a specific and agreed upon agenda that it aggressively pursues. The other side is not in full agreement on any complete set of policies and actions. The Left, therefore, cleverly and effectively depicts the other side as being reactionary and negative in the face of the Left's initiatives.

The United States is facing and must address many problems and threats. Some are economic in nature. Foremost among them is a financial crisis caused, in simple terms, by our government spending money enormously in excess of what it receives. That destructive process is driven, in the opinion of many, by too much earned wealth taken by law from individuals and businesses that create and earn it, and bestowed on those who contribute little or nothing to the economy. Other dangers are posed by implacable and deadly enemies from abroad. The latter include armed conflicts involving American forces in Iraq and Afghanistan, which some on the American Left did not and still do not want us to win; a variety of ruthless Islamic extremists who want to kill us and destroy our property and way of life; a fanatical Iranian regime that is building nuclear weapons, which it or other enemies could use to annihilate our ally, Israel; and the possible acquisition of Pakistan's nuclear arsenal by Islamic jihadists in Afghanistan and Pakistan. Other serious problems are the potential control of our oil supply by foreign powers, from supposed friends like Saudi Arabia to self-declared enemies like Venezuela, who are siphoning our wealth into their bank accounts;

an influx of unskilled illegal immigrants who expect and receive more value—in free education, medical care, and other benefits—than they contribute, and whose presence in our country is encouraged and welcomed by the American Left; cultural crises, in which huge numbers of children are born to young, unmarried parents who do not always support them, and in which millions of people are addicted to or otherwise committed to buying and using illegal drugs; a government-owned, low-quality education system dominated by teachers' unions and inept administrators, which produces young people who cannot think critically or write correctly; an intentionally overcomplicated, expensive, and easily manipulated system of federal taxation, which is used to wield power over us; government-created retirement and health-care systems that will soon be insolvent; *and worst of all, a collection of self-important United States senators and representatives, who see their elected positions as valuable life careers, and who therefore promote their own selfish interests and those of their supporters over the interests of the American people.* The American Left has largely taken over the Democratic Party, which regularly does its bidding. The Republican Party has lost its bearings and courage.

Those issues and more stand between the American people and our ability to deal timely and effectively with aggressions against us and our way of life from an array of foreign enemies. Some of these enemies have declared themselves as such more than others, but they all have in common an implacable hatred of the United States of America and a determination to end our tenure as the most powerful and prosperous nation in the world. Those forces are using terror and stealth attacks against our soldiers in Iraq and Afghanistan and against free people in those and many other countries. They murdered over three thousand innocent people in New York City, the Pentagon, and Pennsylvania on September 11, 2001. That event is now trivialized by some on the Left, which agrees with building an Islamic teaching center six hundred feet from "ground zero," as proposed by an imam who publicly claimed that we helped cause the attacks. Some of our enemies are using the price of oil to advance their interests and drain our wealth. The names of some of our enemies are Iran, Syria, al-Qaeda, Hamas, Hezbollah, Venezuela and its president, Hugo Chavez, Cuba, and North Korea. A major enabler of the Islamic jihadists is our supposed friend, the Kingdom of Saudi Arabia, along with an unknown but large number of its wealthy citizens. China is actively seeking to take our place as the dominant world power. It appears to me that the American Left is tolerant of, and in some cases even supportive of, our enemies.

Unless a one-term limit for senators and representatives, further explained in chapter 3, is adopted, there is no hope that our federal legislators will improve our situation. The critical work they are elected to perform on our behalf has become purely political, with ideology and self-interest displacing reasoned, transparent decision-making based on all available evidence. I believe that too many of our senators and representatives see themselves as the central part of what Professor Angelo M. Codevilla describes as the Ruling Class in his essay, *The Ruling Class*, published in 2010 by Beaufort Books. Codevilla's Ruling Class is a loosely organized group of men, women, and organizations with inflated opinions of their own worth, who believe they should rule the rest of us. With their self-proclaimed superior wisdom, they prescribe how we should act, think, and do business. They take good care of themselves and their allies at the expense of others. Federal legislators with the opportunity for unlimited tenure furnish the legal force for their grand design over the rest of us, the non-ruling class. Given that opportunity and the compulsion of self-interest, few senators and representatives are fit to have a role in determining how our current great struggle unfolds. That is because these members of Congress are primarily interested in being reelected and thus remaining members of Codevilla's Ruling Class. They act to that end, instead of in America's best interests. It is axiomatic that human behavior and the choices humans make are driven by self-interest. No one can legitimately quarrel with that. Citizens will always vote for whom they believe will help them. However, our elected senators and representatives, because of their power and responsibilities, must be held to a different and more elevated standard.

The American people need to become aware of and knowledgeable about the conflict, the issues, and the consequences of a bad outcome. They must make their positions known, taking an active part in the fight. Because America is a republic in which we are represented, for better or worse, by the fellow citizens we elect, it is critical that those we elect be required to act in America's interests, instead of their own.

In the context framed above, let's look at a few things the two sides have done lately.

The Left, which tends to control the Democrats in each house, has since World War II shrunk from the use of force to advance American interests. It seeks to appease or bribe, but not defeat, America's enemies. It has difficulty distinguishing between allies and enemies. For example, in 2009 our government, seemingly to please Russia, which is not our ally, reneged on our commitment to place missile defenses in Poland and the Czech Republic, both staunch allies of the United States. What possible, legitimate reason could Russia have to oppose strategic measures intended solely to shoot down incoming warheads? If someone pressures you to become defenseless, don't you need to ask why? Iran, an obvious enemy, is well on its way to having nuclear weapons and becoming a dominant hostile power in the Middle East. During the riots in Iran in 2009 protesting President Mahmoud Ahmadinejad's seemingly rigged reelection, our leaders chose to say and do nothing to support the opposition. Yet in early 2011, when protesters filled the streets of Cairo and other cities of our important ally, Egypt, our government supported the protests and called for President Mubarak to step aside. The Left's (and our current government's) solution to the problem of atomic warheads in Iranian hands rules out force in favor of endless talks and a series of "sanctions" that have been ineffective. In 2009 Secretary of State Hillary Clinton, as reported on July 23, 2009, in the *Wall Street Journal*, "caused waves in the Middle East" by publicly stating in Thailand that the United States "could extend a 'defense umbrella' to protect its Arab allies if Iran succeeds in developing nuclear weapons." Our leaders seem more interested in imposing debilitating conditions on our democratic ally, Israel, such as pressing it to relinquish control of territory from which hostile forces can then fire rockets at its cities, than in using any means needed to stop our enemy, Iran, from having a nuclear arsenal.

Even more confounding, our government has intentionally downgraded Great Britain as our ally and friend. For example, Secretary of State Clinton, in a press conference in Buenos Aires on March 2, 2010, with Argentine President Cristina Kirchner, told Kirchner and the world that Britain, which won a costly and bloody war with Argentina in 1982 to hold the Falkland Islands, should now negotiate with Argentina over the future of that British territory and its primarily British inhabitants.[1]

Domestically, between January 2009 and the end of 2010, the Left, with Democratic majorities in the Senate and House, gave the federal government dramatically increased control over American industry, including small businesses. Some examples are laws on banking and finance (enacted), health care (enacted), and limits on industrial emissions coupled with financial penalties for emissions deemed excessive (passed the House). Others are legislative approval of massive sequential financial aid with our money, much of it borrowed, to businesses selected by our leaders, which many believe should have failed or undergone court-supervised reorganization. In my opinion, those laws and spending measures, including but not limited to the bailouts of General Motors and Chrysler, each engineered to favor the United Auto Workers, were driven more by ideology than by carefully reasoned decision making based on evidence and experience.

While the national election in November 2010 was a repudiation of leftist domestic policies, I am not confident that the other side can or will do better. Its proxies, after all, are also committed to being reelected.

Republicans made and then broke the Contract with America that brought them to congressional power in 1994. They promised the

1 Nile Gardiner, "Hillary Clinton Slaps Britain in the Face over the Falklands," *World*, March 2, 2010, accessed June 10, 2011, http:blogs.telegraph.co.uk/news/nilegardiner/100028048/Hillary-clinton-slaps-britain-in-the-face.

American people a new and better program, but then served their own interests instead of keeping their promises. This was a collective act of infamy. President George W. Bush was a more patriotic leader and a more determined promoter of America's vital interests than Al Gore or John Kerry would have been, but in my opinion he was in many ways an indecisive and ineffective leader. For example, he invaded Iraq on evidence that turned out to be flawed, yet did nothing of consequence about Iran for eight years, even though Iran furnished lethal weapons to our enemies in Iraq and made enormous progress in developing a nuclear arsenal. Bush allowed Congressional spending to reach wild excesses, when he could have used his veto to curb them. He was in office for nearly two full terms "before he had the guts to veto a spending bill because it cost too much."[2] Republican legislators were a big factor in those excesses. That makes them doubly culpable, since they were elected on promises of fiscal conservatism. Bush also inexplicably allowed his marginal rate reductions in the federal income tax and his estate tax relief to be temporary rather than permanent, glaring errors that he had time to fix while his party controlled Congress. He instead wasted his time and political capital on a doomed plan to partially privatize Social Security. Bush allowed a war we could have easily won to become a disastrous occupation, partly due to wrong decisions and partly due to massive opposition from the American Left. When he had the means to do so, he failed to push for the building of new nuclear power plants, new oil refineries, and domestic oil exploration and extraction in easily accessible areas. We need all of these things, lest we continue transferring our wealth to our oil-rich enemies. Had he done those things when his party controlled Congress, our energy crisis would by now be less severe.

Legislators in both parties use federal taxation as a means of controlling industrial and social policy instead of for its intended and limited purpose of funding the federal government. Republicans and Democrats in both houses have not dealt with the upcoming insolvency

2 Tara L. Tedrow, "Young Conservative: GOP Betrays Me," *Orlando Sentinel*, February 9, 2008.

of Social Security for two reasons. First, they misappropriated and spent the Social Security money on other programs; and second, the only real solution, as I propose in chapter 14, would be unpopular and jeopardize their tenure.

I wrote *American Manifesto* in the hope that Americans will take from it that it is we, not politicians, who must act. Too often any action a politician takes is mainly for his or her benefit. Recent history provides examples of effective action by ordinary people that influenced public policy. Bush's nomination of Harriet Miers to the Supreme Court was a foolish blunder. The American people rose up and erased it. Bush awoke and appointed an experienced federal appellate judge, Samuel Alito. Bush urged an immigration bill that would have legalized millions of illegal immigrants, and encouraged the continuation of the flood of unskilled and poor immigrants, while discouraging the immigration of educated and skilled immigrants. The bill also would have done nothing to enforce existing immigration law. The American people took care of that as well. It can be done.

The first and most essential thing to be done is to remove the selfish motives our elected legislators have to continue to hold office, *and the only way to do that is to deprive them of the opportunity of self-succession*. That would jump-start the process of solving the problems and overcoming the threats discussed in this book. Our nation must cease being governed and led by self-perpetuating, self-promoting, and self-serving federal legislators. We must elect senators and representatives who act in our interests, not their own. We need such individuals to believe in and to act upon the foundations of a love of America, moral clarity, personal accountability, self-reliance, common sense, and old-fashioned honor. And we and our elected legislators need to get serious about defending America and its position in the world, regardless of opposition from within.

CHAPTER 2

Micawber's Advice on Financial Responsibility

In 1850 Charles Dickens published *David Copperfield*. Its relevance to *American Manifesto* stems from advice given to the main character, David, by his older friend, Wilkins Micawber. I quote the advice in full: "'My other piece of advice, Copperfield,' said Mr. Micawber, 'you know. Annual income twenty pounds, annual expenditure nineteen six, result happiness. Annual income twenty pounds, annual expenditure twenty pounds ought and six, result misery. The blossom is blighted, the leaf is withered, the god of day goes down upon the dreary scene, and—and in short you are forever floored. As I am!'"[3] Mr. Micawber spoke the obvious truth that if a household, a business entity, or a nation spends more money than it earns or otherwise legitimately receives, the result is economic collapse and other disasters and hardships which attend that.

I do not presume to know how many of our current federal lawmakers have read *David Copperfield*. But I do know that the majority of them have little regard for the timeless and axiomatic lesson propounded by Micawber, which is that living within one's means tends to generate prosperity and happiness; and that spending,

3 Charles Dickens, *David Copperfield* (New York: Bantam Books, 1981), 162.

whether by actual outlays of money or by borrowing in excess of what one earns or otherwise collects places the spender on an inexorable path to catastrophe and disgrace. Because of profligate government spending and borrowing by previous federal legislators of both parties, as well as the current Congress, in all cases tolerated or encouraged by successive presidents, the greatest nation the world has known is at the tipping point of economic disaster.

A dire forecast of that sounded on April 18, 2011, when Standard & Poor's publicly warned that there was a one in three chance of a downgrade in the AAA credit rating of the United States as early as 2013.[4] A downgrade could raise borrowing costs for the government, business entities, and individuals. S&P stated that "about half of public U.S. debt is held by foreigners," making the situation more perilous.[5] Then, on August 5, 2011, Standard & Poor's downgraded our credit rating from AAA to AA+. Standard & Poor's placed responsibility for the downgrade on Congress.[6] It further stated that the unsolved debt problem of the United States and the "nature of the debate [in Congress] and the difficulty in framing a political consensus" were the key considerations.[7]

A frightening statistic is that United States' federal debt has risen from about $8 trillion in 2006 to about $15.5 trillion in 2011.[8] Another is that federal debt as a percentage of gross domestic product (the aggregate value of all goods and services produced in a year) rose from about 60 percent in 2006 to about 90 percent in 2010, and is estimated

---

4 "U.S. Could Lose AAA Rating by 2013 without Budget Deal, S&P Says," *Investor's Business Daily*, April 19, 2011.

5 Ibid.

6 Frank Byrt, "S&P Blames Inept Congress for Downgrades," *The Street*, August 8, 2011, accessed August 8, 2011, *http://www.thestreet.com/story/11213656/1/sp-blames-inept-congress-for-downgrade.html?cm-ven+GOOGLEN.*

7 Elise Foley, "S&P Officials Blame Downgrade on 'Degree of Uncertainty' In Politics," *HuffPost Business*, August 7, 2011, *http://www.huffingtonpost.com/2011/08/07/standard-and-poors-downgrade-defense-politics_n_920430.html.*

8 *www.usgovernmentspending.com/federal_debt_chart.html*, accessed April 26, 2011.

to exceed 100 percent in 2012![9] That is not surprising, as each day the federal government borrows another $4.1 billion, more than $2 million per minute![10] The interest on that is about $616 million per day.[11]

How can this have happened? A liberal columnist, Robert Samuelson, wrote that "We have created suicidal government," meaning that "government has promised more than it can deliver and, as a result, repeatedly disappoints by providing less than people expect or jeopardizing what they already have."[12] Samuelson wrote that government cannot "easily correct its excesses because Americans depend on it for so much that any effort to change the status quo arouses a firestorm of opposition that virtually ensures defeat."[13] The latter observation is confirmed by occurrences at a town hall meeting held in Orlando on April 26, 2011, by Representative Daniel Webster, elected in 2010 on a platform that he would press for reduced spending and a reduced deficit. Webster, while trying to explain why spending must be reduced, was heckled and insulted by attendees who were irate at the notion of changes in Medicare.[14] In my view, this is evidence that government policies are changing people from being reliant on their own abilities and efforts into a "nation of takers."[15] The angry attendees at Webster's meeting are not entirely unlike the thousands of violent demonstrators in Greece, who are so conditioned to being supported by government that they cannot peacefully accept the austerity measures required to avoid a ruinous economic collapse.

In the United States, the overspending and overborrowing threaten to continue. A May 20, 2011, article states that in 1945 (the end of

9 Ibid.

10 Senator John Barrasso, "Needed: Fiscal Leadership, Not PR Stunts," *Investor's Business Daily*, May 12, 2011.

11 Ibid.

12 Robert J. Samuelson, "Big Gov't Edges Ever Closer to Self-Destruction," On the Left, *Investor's Business Daily*, April 11, 2011.

13 Ibid.

14 Mark Schlueb, "Webster Gets an Earful at Rowdy Town-Hall Meeting," *Orlando Sentinel*, April 27, 2011.

15 Scott A. Hodge, "Once Self-Reliant, Now a Nation of Takers," *Investor's Business Daily*, April 8, 2010.

World War II), in 1970, and again in 1990, all very different times in our history, the average percentage of gross domestic product that our government took in taxes was 18 percent. However, in the ten-year budget being proposed as of June 2011 by the current administration, the percentage of GDP the government wants to spend is 24 percent! [16] The Congressional Budget Office projected what the country's financial situation will be if we pursue anything similar to that spending and borrowing course. Taxes would be between 19.25 and 26 percent of GDP, "spending would eclipse 45% of GDP" (due to Social Security, Medicare, and Obamacare), and our national debt would "skyrocket" to unprecedented levels, to almost 350 percent of GDP.[17] "Federal health programs alone would eat up more than three-quarters of our historic levels of taxation."[18]

In my opinion, Micawber's advice to young Copperfield illuminates the critical key to saving America from destruction inflicted by its own federal lawmakers and its creditors, foreign and otherwise. In contrast to Micawber's modest overexpenditures, our nation, on average, *spends $125 billion per month in excess of what it takes in.*[19] Micawber faced debtors' prison, a grim prospect in 1850. Our great nation is faced with much worse: an economic collapse and consequent social disaster that will materially diminish our standard of living and lower our standing among nations. In my opinion, the spending and borrowing versus GDP discussed in the Anderson article, a course to which the current US government seems committed, will cause our great nation to undergo the bankruptcy-like economic collapses suffered by Chile in 1973, the Soviet Union in 1991, Argentina in 2001, and Greece in 2011.[20] If our economy goes that way, if we do not stop spending and borrowing more than we earn, we may end up humiliated by having

16 Jeffrey H. Anderson, "Economic Destiny Comes down to Obama vs. Ryan," *Investor's Business Daily*, May 20, 2011.

17 Ibid.

18 Ibid.

19 Lisa Mascaro and Kathleen Hennessy, "Boehner's Plan: Cut 'Trillions,'" *Orlando Sentinel*, May 10, 2011.

20 "Greece, and Us," *Investor's Business Daily*, July 1, 2011.

to take orders from the likes of China, Russia, and Iran. At the same time, our currency may collapse, our credit rating may be destroyed, and all of us, including leftist elites, may live closer to poverty than we can now imagine.

Who can prevent the foregoing? Notwithstanding decades of ritualistic criticism of presidents for overspending and creating deficits, taxation, government spending, and balancing the budget are exclusively the province of Congress.[21] Presidents with socialistic leanings do not help, but Congress controls whether we follow Mr. Micawber's advice or act as he did. That is because Article I, Section 7 of the Constitution grants Congress the exclusive power to levy taxes. The President can ask, but has no authority to raise or lower taxes.[22] The same applies to federal spending. A president cannot spend any money that federal legislators do not first appropriate. Nonetheless, when presidents get blamed for overtaxing and overspending, it makes Congress look less blameworthy. Wrote Professor Williams, "Of course, if you're a congressman, not being held accountable is what you want."[23] This tells you a lot about why *American Manifesto* focuses on Congress, not the presidency.

As of late 2011, what have our federal lawmakers been doing about this increasingly critical problem? You guessed it—little or nothing, other than hurling accusations back and forth in efforts to keep themselves from being replaced in the next election. Even the new Republican Senate and House members elected in 2010 on promises of fiscal restraint and financial accountability managed only a statistically meaningless reduction in federal spending in early 2011. It is somewhat encouraging that House Republicans sought to negotiate some reductions in spending in exchange for agreeing to raise the federal debt ceiling. It is deeply disheartening, however, that that issue of increasing the government's line of credit is even before Congress,

21 Walter Williams, "Fault Congress, Not President, for Federal Budget Problems," *Investor's Business Daily*, March 15, 2011.

22 Ibid.

23 Ibid.

and more so that the Senate majority and House minority oppose meaningful spending reductions. And, as of late 2011, the collective efforts to raise the limit and stave off an alleged default were less about finding a solution and more about manipulating public opinion in efforts to affect the next election. There can be no better example of self-interest superseding the public interest.

It is pointless, however, to rail against the lawmakers as being bad people, and it is impossible to expect them to perform differently. They are human, and their conduct is based on human nature and self-interest. It would be good if we had a race of enlightened, selfless statesmen and women to serve, but we do not. That is the essence of why I advocate the one-term limit. In my considered opinion, the United States has a good chance of self-destruction and second-tier status in the world without it.

CHAPTER 3

Human Character and American Federal Lawmakers: The Solution Explained

Kenneth Roberts stated in his magnificent 1933 historical novel, *Rabble in Arms*, which chronicles the travails and exploits of our Northern Army in our war for independence, that his writing would not please "such innocents who are convinced that men in public office always set the nation's welfare above their own."[24] This problem to which Roberts refers has gotten increasingly worse, to the point of being out of control.

The United States is a supposedly democratic republic governed by elected officials, most of them in legislative bodies. Those who are doing the greatest damage to our nation are United States senators and members of the House of Representatives. That is especially true of those who hold positions of special power in the Senate and House. The Speaker of the House of Representatives, the Majority Leader of the Senate, and the chairs of the major committees in both bodies wield near-dictatorial power over their colleagues, and thus over us. They control the voting of their party members because that keeps them in

24 Kenneth Roberts, *Rabble in Arms: A Chronicle of Arundel and the Burgoyne Invasion* (Garden City, New York: Doubleday & Company, Inc., 1948), 1.

office, and the subordinate party members obey because they believe doing so ensures their own tenure.

Has it ever occurred to you how incongruous it is that the president of the United States, by reason of the Twenty-second Amendment to the Constitution, passed in Congress in 1947 and ratified in 1951, can serve only two terms, while senators and representatives have no such limits? They can serve as long as they continue being elected. Further, there is some transparency to the presidency. Presidents, who are limited to eight years in office, tend to react to criticism of their policies. Members of the House and Senate, however, short of a crime or serious ethical lapse, can do pretty much whatever they want. It is difficult to hold them accountable for their actions because of the enormous advantages of incumbency, which include name recognition, money, and mass mailings at our expense. According to the Center for Responsive Politics, between 1964 and 2010 the reelection rates of House incumbents were between 85 percent and 98 percent; and of Senate incumbents, between 55 percent (in 1980, the "Reagan Revolution") and 96 percent (twice). The Center attributes such success to name recognition and "an insurmountable advantage in campaign cash." In addition to those built-in advantages, to ensure being reelected, federal lawmakers say, do, and spend whatever it takes to remain in power. Whether their conduct serves our best interest is a secondary consideration at best. This is the main contributor to the problems our nation faces, and may lead to its downfall.

Few men or women, having acquired power, are agreeable to relinquishing it, and many will go to extremes to retain it. Dictators the world over are and have been willing to wreck their countries' economies and jail and kill their fellow citizens so that they can remain in power. Fidel Castro and Robert Mugabe are living examples. Cuba and Rhodesia (now called Zimbabwe) had thriving economies before those two took control, yet to this day Castro and Mugabe, each of whom is as good as dead, imprison or kill opponents who threaten their holds on power. Hugo Chavez and Venezuela are well along the same disastrous course. Chavez wants to emulate the late Francois "Papa

Doc" Duvalier of Haiti by being President for Life. But look what has happened to Haiti, a desperate and ruined society. More recently, in early 2011 the Libyan ruler, Muammar Gadhafi, went to war against his own people, killing thousands, to remain in power. The destruction and devastation since the late 1950s of various countries in Africa and the accompanying millions of deaths from starvation and murder, accompanied in some cases by horrific mutilations, are in large part the result of elected leaders more interested in clinging to power than in the welfare of their nations and the people in them. Sir Edward Gibbon, in *The Decline and Fall of the Roman Empire*, first published in 1776, attributed the fall of Rome as much to the centuries-long practice of Roman leaders, both political and military, of killing off their most accomplished rivals as to the increasing decadence of Roman society. Long before Gibbon, William Shakespeare thought that theme important enough to devote a whole play, *Julius Caesar*, to the story of the needless murder of one of Rome's greatest leaders.

In our own country, Bill Clinton and his supporters placed our vital affairs on hold for more than a year while they fought his impeachment for perjury, obstruction of justice, and malfeasance in office, which stemmed from his sexual misconduct while on duty in the Oval Office. It is thus not surprising that in the cases of some of our United States senators and representatives, decisions that are critical to our future are being made almost exclusively on the basis of self-interest.

The nature of human character can be endlessly debated. Humans are capable of mass homicide for political or personal gain, barbaric torture of other humans for enjoyment, and mass enslavement of humans for reasons of conquest, wealth, or sex. (If you don't believe the latter, read about the Japanese conquests of China and Korea in World War II and the practice of sex slavery.) Compared to that sort of behavior, elected politicians' lying to constituents and selling votes in order to hang on to power and glory is trivial (although not inconsequential). Humans are also capable of acts of unsolicited kindness, uncompensated generosity, and sacrifice, as well as of creating great literature and works of music and art. God's gift of the ability to reason and remember is a blessing, but it can also be a curse, because he lets us make choices.

Modern Americans place supreme value on money, power, and celebrity. Being elected to Congress is a good way to get all of those. The longer a person remains in office, the more power he or she obtains, and the greater the potential for wealth. In Revolutionary times, serving in Congress was a good way to get killed or to lose your money, property, friends, and family. The one thing our Founding Fathers, faced as they were with potential ruin and death, could not have anticipated was how attractive and addictive it would later become to serve in Congress. Now, being in the Senate or House is a sweet deal, involving no risk and huge rewards. Senators and House members have great health care and fabulous retirement benefits, all funded by money they take from us. They gave themselves a pay raise during the worst recession in modern times, while publicly and hypocritically excoriating talented and productive private-sector executives for being well-paid and receiving bonuses. Some multiterm senators and congressmen retire and become wealthy influence peddlers in law or lobbying firms, write books, give paid speeches, and make huge sums of money. Many of them, like the late Ted Kennedy, Senator John Kerry, and former Senator John Edwards, not unlike other persons of great wealth, have complex tax avoidance schemes. Even worse, long-term incumbents, while working on our payroll, build up truly gigantic sums of cash for future campaigns, while challengers must start raising funds on their own time from a zero base.

The unsettling and corrupting factor is that to remain in office, senators and representatives have to convince others to vote for them. That requires a lot of time, effort, and money. Sadly, it is usually not done by acting in a statesmanlike fashion and in the best interests of the United States. It is instead done by using the power of office to do four things: One is to tell voters whatever half-truth or lie is necessary to acquire their money and their votes. Another is either to vote for or against important legislation solely to please supporters and campaign contributors. The third is a practice never contemplated by the founders of our republic—the use of federal tax funds for projects of purely local interest in the congresspeople's home districts. Votes enabling that wasteful practice are traded like marbles on a playground. For example, as reported on June 27, 2009, in the *Orlando Sentinel*, former Florida Representative Alan Grayson sold his vote for the Cap and Trade bill in exchange for a promise of support for an unnecessary Hurricane Research Center in his district.[25] The fourth, and worst, is the use of federal taxation as an instrument to reward supporters and promote their causes, and to deprive, punish, or marginalize the opponents of those supporters. If a congressman does not do all of those things, he probably will serve only one term and lose his power and the promise of personal gain.

The corruptibility of members of Congress crosses party lines. Republican or Democrat, there is simply too much to gain by serving multiple terms. Thus, the behavior of federal legislators is overtly and covertly self-serving, not to mention wasteful. Too many elected politicians act in their own best interests, not those of their country, and conceal their motives by duplicity and lying. Hollywood mogul David Geffen was not just talking about the Clintons when he said that all politicians lie. Geffen, a one-time Clinton supporter, said that all politicians lie but, as chronicled on CBS News on February 21, 2009, he added that the Clintons do so with "such ease." Self-interest is a key part of the genetic makeup of all of us. Due to self-interest, many individuals act duplicitously and selfishly, but it damages the country when elected politicians use the power of their positions to do so.

The unavoidable conclusion is that the self-interest of Senate and House members leads to their votes being controlled and driven by others, either by the individuals or groups that helped them get elected or by party bosses who are similarly obligated. From January 2009 on, we have witnessed the most blatant political paybacks ever seen in our country. Legislation authorizing unprecedented spending, including

25 Heath Whiteaker, "Storm Brewing Over New Hurricane Center," *Central Florida Politics.com*, August 12, 2009, accessed February 28, 2011, http://centralfloridapolitics.com/tag/cap-and-trade.

clandestine spending on local projects, was rushed to passage on the dubious claim that emergency conditions required it. The "emergency" made it necessary, in the opinion of our elected representatives, to pass legislation that would allow spending gigantic amounts of money over an indefinite period. The timing was such that the legislation could not have been read by everyone who voted for it. All dissent was shouted down and suppressed. Politicians who knew better told monstrous lies about the cost of the legislation. No disinterested person can claim this was anything other than payback for the election of Democrats. Thus, self-interest of our lawmakers trumps national interest, to the great detriment of the United States of America.

While the American people should be the ones who decide the course of our nation, our form of representative government requires that elected federal legislators perform the actual decision making by casting formal votes. The fact, however, that we are a republic does not mean that we are required to have self-interested and self-serving career legislators who skew their decision making to please their supporters and preserve their power. Other than changing our form of government to a monarchy or a dictatorship, which is not an option, there is only one solution. *That is, the strict limit of one term per person, with no opportunity to ever again run for a seat in either chamber.*

The Constitution prescribes that members of the House of Representatives be "chosen every second Year by the People of the several States" and that the Senate shall consist of two Senators from each state "elected by the people thereof, for six years." Because the document is silent on term limits for representatives and senators, they have long indulged themselves in as many terms as possible. Ted Kennedy was in the Senate for forty-six years. The late Robert Byrd was there fifty-one years, running for a ninth term at age eighty-eight. Strom Thurmond, who served forty-nine years, was still in office at one hundred years of age. A legally unassailable term limit for federal lawmakers would require an amendment to the Constitution. If a 1951 amendment could limit the most powerful elected official in the world to two terms, we should be able to limit our self-important federal legislative potentates to one. I suggest dispensing with the two-year and six-year terms and replacing them with a single four-year term for each United States senator and representative, with no opportunity to run again for either chamber. The terms would be staggered, with a nationwide election held every two years. Incumbents would be barred from selecting their successors in any way, including giving away unused campaign funds. Rather, those funds would be returned to donors.

If senators and representatives knew they would only serve one term in one legislative body, many good things would happen. An important one is that persons of the lowest character and most given to greed and venality would not bother to run, because of the lack of sufficient opportunities for self-aggrandizement, power, and wealth. A corollary is that more truly capable men and women would run, and fewer incompetent ones would. The former would have track records of success in the real world, and the confidence that they could pick up where they left off after their four years of service. Another good thing is that those elected would tend not to be driven by the hope of any wealth derived from office, since four years is not long enough to build much of a following. Another is that because they would know they would have to return to private life and earn a living, they would be motivated to maintain a sterling reputation. "Nothing so strongly impels a man to regard the interest of his constituents, as the certainty of returning to the general mass of the people, from whence he was taken, where he must participate in their burdens."[26] That factor would motivate incumbents not to burden the American economy with unnecessary taxation and regulation, since each one-termer would be returning to the private sector. The main thing, however, is that they would be independent of the powerful influences that now control federal legislative decision-making.

Under the present system, incumbent senators and representatives spend large amounts of their paid time while in office, as well as government money, on campaigning. No other employment allows

---

26 George Mason, speech at Virginia Ratifying Convention, June 17, 1788.

a person to pursue his own interests while working for someone else, not to mention to spend his employer's money in the process. With the one-term limit, the only campaigning would take place before the first and only term. Those campaigns would take place on the candidates' time, not ours. Our money would not be used against us in campaigns by incumbents running for reelection. Money, relentlessly and endlessly solicited by incumbent federal lawmakers from all available sources and received by them in huge sums, is the controlling factor in most federal legislative races. That money is solicited while the incumbents should be doing their jobs, and it is paid to influence the way in which their jobs are done. A recent CNN/Opinion Research Corporation survey found that 86 percent of the public thinks federal lawmakers "are mostly influenced by pressure from contributors."[27] Imagine the improvement in the quality and quantity of the work of the House and Senate if members were not constantly fundraising and campaigning! Because there would be no incumbents running, with little or no personal reward at stake, and no reason for special interests to lavish money on candidates, campaigns would cost a fraction of what they cost now. Campaign finance laws might cease to be needed. Campaigns would involve less lying, because non-incumbents would not have pre-established constituencies open to being persuaded by lies, half-truths, and distortions.

Recent history includes one offensive practice our lawmakers engage in that would cease. That is the unnecessary and unproductive ritualistic flogging in public hearings of private sector executives, such as the CEOs of the major auto companies, the largest banks, and major oil companies. Such activities serve no purpose other than political, and to curry favor with a public that seems to enjoy seeing successful businesspeople brutalized by mediocre men and women who happen to hold elected office.

Another consequence of the one-term limit would be that party leaders, such as the Senate Majority Leader and the Speaker of the

---

27 Tom Hamburger, "The Power of Money," *Orlando Sentinel*, June 9, 2011.

House, would not be able to extort votes on legislation from their parties' members by granting or withholding support for the next election. Nor is it likely that they would marshal outside forces to visit states or districts to defeat opposing party candidates. Examples of that occurred in 2008 and 2010 in Minnesota, when Nancy Pelosi in 2008 and Bill Clinton in 2010 campaigned there against Congresswoman Michele Bachmann.

The fact that voting on important legislation takes place along rigid party lines is evidence that such voting is driven in part by compulsion and bribery as practiced by party leaders. Republicans and Democrats do, after all, have minds. One would think that, absent control by party bosses, there would be more crossing of party lines on important, highly publicized proposed legislation. Examples from 2010 of votes obtained by combinations of bribery and coercion are the votes on the Patient Protection and Affordable Care Act of 2010 ("Obamacare") by senators from Vermont, Nebraska, Louisiana, Florida, Connecticut, and Montana in obvious exchange for special financial concessions to their states or to special interests therein.[28] In those transactions, the participants committed acts which in the private sector could have gotten them indicted. Under a one-term limit, senators and representatives would be less prone to practice what is euphemistically called partisanship. In reality, partisanship is a relentless and destructive battle between parties, which forces voting along party lines instead of in accordance with rational and evidence-based decision making. If you are in office for only one term, the party's or its leaders' positions on the issues are not controlling. You are there for your country's business, not to advance the interests of a political party or those to whom it is indebted. One-term legislators would have little concern for how party bosses wanted them to vote.

The proposition that federal legislators are desperate to remain in office is proven by many things in addition to their shameless, supporter-driven voting. First and foremost, previous initiatives to limit

28 David Freddoso, *Gangster Government* (Washington, D.C.: Regnery Publishing, Inc., 2011), 71-72.

terms, all of which, to my knowledge, allowed more than one term, were and remain anathema to incumbent legislators. Second, legislative candidates who campaign on a promise to serve a limited number of terms typically find reasons to break those promises. Third, and most cynical of all, elected officials resort to lawyers and the courts to set aside term limit legislation when they can find a pliable judge willing to take such action. There can be no act more arrogant than asking a judge to set aside term limit legislation that was enacted by a duly elected legislature. That takes a special kind of cynicism.

Let's look at a few cases of politicians who, having the power and advantages of incumbency, acted in their own interests to the detriment of our country. In each case, I contend that those who controlled the House of Representatives or the Senate either took action or prevented action to please a powerful group of supporters. In each case, the best interests of the United States suffered.

Former Speaker of the House Nancy Pelosi committed nation-endangering malfeasance in 2008 by not allowing a vote for many months on the Foreign Intelligence Surveillance Act (FISA). FISA permits federal agents to listen to telephone conversations between suspected foreign terrorists and persons within our borders. One reason Pelosi delayed the vote on the legislation, now passed, is that it contained legal protection for telecommunications companies that cooperate with federal agents. The telecommunications companies are not legally required to help the government, and are reluctant to cooperate without legal protection. However, trial lawyers have made enormous sums of money from suing such companies, and spent some of that money supporting Pelosi. It is reasonable to suspect that one reason why this legislation was blocked was because the trial lawyers did not want it passed. Another reason was that well-funded groups on the Left, like George Soros's MoveOn.org, seem to me to oppose the entire concept of protecting our shores. Such groups give enormous sums to candidates who support their causes and spend money to punish those who do not. Pelosi's behavior in this matter was a dangerous and irresponsible abuse of power, and was apparently motivated by obligations to those two wealthy groups.

Another example is the trade agreement the George W. Bush administration negotiated in 2006 with Colombia. Colombia is one of our important democratic allies on a continent in which formerly friendly nations like Bolivia have turned socialist and hostile to America. The socialist president of Venezuela, Hugo Chavez, reviled President Bush and has openly declared his wish to conquer Colombia. He has furnished millions of dollars to the leftist guerillas, the Revolutionary Armed Forces of Colombia (FARC), which operate on the borders of Colombia, Venezuela, and Ecuador. FARC would like to overthrow the Colombian government and is a source of illegal drugs sold and used in our country. Chavez's complicity with these international criminals was proven by computer records seized by the Colombian military after a raid on a FARC camp in Ecuador.[29] More recently, Chavez publicly insulted President Barack Obama and has made arms deals with Iran and Russia.

The proposed trade agreement would significantly augment the prosperity of Colombia at a time when it is desperately needed and would secure it from being overcome by Chavez and his Russia-furnished weapons. Its ratification by Congress would demonstrate that America supports democratic governments that fight narco-terrorists, not socialists like Chavez and President Evo Morales of Bolivia, both declared enemies of our country and supporters of FARC. The treaty would also help American businesses and create employment during tough economic times. Its non-ratification might mean the end of similar agreements, a consequence that would harm our economy. Non-ratification has cost us jobs and money and is allowing other countries, such as Canada, to reap benefits that could have been available to us. No matter: American labor unions don't want the trade agreement to pass. For that reason, Pelosi abrogated a longstanding House rule that required a vote on trade bills within ninety days of submittal to Congress

29 Oliver North, "A Despot's Distraction," *Real Clear Politics* (March 7, 2008).

by the president.[30] Thanks to Pelosi's unprecedented manipulation of the rule and her obeisance to labor union bosses, the bill remained in limbo until after the 2008 election. Labor unions rejoiced that the new president was a Democrat and might not resubmit the legislation. Indeed, the 2006 agreement languished until September, 2011, to the increasing detriment of United States cattle and wheat exporters.[31]

Labor unions should not be in a position to dictate American foreign policy. The labor unions have stated that Colombia has not done enough to curb abuses toward labor union leaders in Colombia. That is not, however, the case. Nor is it the reason. The real reason is that American labor unions are against all trade agreements because, in their ignorance, they think such agreements cause a net loss of American jobs. Pelosi and her colleagues do their bidding because labor unions are some of the biggest contributors to their campaigns. Without labor unions, most House and Senate Democrats would not be in office.

A third case involves Senate Majority Leader Harry Reid loudly telling the world that we had lost the Iraq War, when in fact we were winning, and senators like Hillary Clinton calling General David Petraeus, who helped win the war, a liar when he reported to the Senate on Iraq War issues. Reid and Clinton wanted to placate and please the American Left,[32] regardless of harm to the war effort and the risk to our fighting men and women. No group, however wealthy, should be able to induce senators to commit such acts.

More recent cases of vote-buying legislative action are the so-called stimulus package, the bailouts of General Motors Corporation and Chrysler Corporation, and the House-passed legislation commonly known as the Cap and Trade bill. The stimulus package was rushed through both chambers in early 2009 on a purported emergency basis by Democratic leadership. Considering the complexity of the bill and the short time legislators had to review it, I wonder how many of them

---

30 "Pelosi's War," *Investor's Business Daily*, April 11, 2008.

31 "Baucus' Beefs," *Investor's Business Daily*, January 31, 2011.

32 Remember MoveOn.org's September 10, 2007, full-page ad in the *New York Times* on "General Betray Us"?

had time to read it and fully understand it. The country was told that emergency measures were needed, that President Obama and his appointees knew best, and that everyone needed to be quiet and submit. Conservatives who pointed out the massive amounts of pork in the stimulus legislation were demonized and insulted by President Obama and the House and Senate leadership.

The Cap and Trade bill was passed by the House by a six-vote majority, on the increasingly disputed premise that global warming exists and that carbon dioxide gas emitted by industry causes it. Evidence offered by experts that the legislation would destroy hundreds of thousands of American jobs, diminish our gross domestic product, and give China and India—two major polluters who have refused to agree to any emission standards—a damaging competitive advantage was ignored. Those who offered such evidence were told to shut up. The same was true for those who showed that the effect of the law on world temperatures would be *de minimis*. Again, the legislators did not have time to read the legislation, which is about as thick as a big-city telephone book.[33] Democratic leadership told us that the debate on global warming is over, and that immediate passage of this bill was necessary to save the planet. At the same time, a leading proponent of global warming, former Vice President Al Gore, has steadfastly refused to debate scientists who assert, based on evidence, that industrial emissions do not cause global warming and that the planet is actually cooling. (A court in England barred Gore's film on global warming from being shown at schools without an accompanying warning about misstatements and misinformation.) Those who spoke out against Cap and Trade from knowledge instead of ideology, who argued that the legislation would cause irreparable harm to the American economy, were shoved aside and ridiculed.

In the cases of General Motors and Chrysler, the money loaned and given to them was directed first and foremost to benefit the United Auto Workers, the union that represents their employees. The UAW, if

33 Editorial, "Closing the Books on the Worst Congress", *Washington Examiner,* December 25, 2010.

a creditor at all, was an unsecured creditor, last in line under the law. The UAW, however, which had a leading role in electing Obama and the then-Democrat majorities in the House and Senate, was unlawfully favored over secured creditors in direct defiance of the Bankruptcy Act. The UAW became a major owner of the two companies.[34]

The point here is not to debate the merits of these subjects, but to identify them as examples of critical issues that should have been decided by lawmakers on the basis of empirical evidence, not on ideology, and without aggressive, scorched-earth tactics toward opposing views. Each such decision should have been made only after careful study by unbiased, disinterested, and noncoerced legislators, and not rushed through by paper-thin majorities that were taking orders from Barack Obama, Nancy Pelosi, Harry Reid, Al Gore, powerful billionaires of dubious loyalty, and other elements of the American Left.

There is no valid reason not to restrict a senator or representative to one term, apart from selfish reasons of incumbents. These positions were never meant to be careers. Employment in any other field can be terminated by either party at any time. Why should federal legislators be allowed to buy sequential terms with our money? For an elected federal legislator, a long, multiterm career is a career in self-service. Human nature has not changed since ancient times. The only thing that can force elected legislators to act and vote other than in their own interests, or in the interests of those who keep them in power, is a single term short enough to remove self-interest from consideration.

There are three plausible arguments against a one-term limit.

First, the legislator, being obligated to no one, would be accountable to no one other than himself. The answers to that are, first, that is unavoidable; and second, it's part of the plan. A parliamentary republic is not a utopia operated by gods. Voters and lawmakers will still make mistakes. There just will not be as many mistakes, nor will they be of a self-perpetuating nature.

Another argument is that powerful one-issue groups could still

34 Freddoso, *Gangster Government*, 17-51.

attempt to place and influence their own candidates, if only for a single term. Such attempts, however, would be more difficult and a lot less effective in cases of candidates not yet in office, and with no certainty they will even get there. Further, even multiterm legislators, if they can get away with it, break their promises to supporters. Once in office, one-termers with outstanding obligations to supporters would be free to repudiate such debts unless bribery were in play. In that regard, no serious person claims that all human wrongdoing can be eliminated. It can, however, be greatly diminished.

The third argument is fatuous, but will be made: "It's always been that way, it's just politics." Nonsense. Even if that is factually correct, which is dubious, the problem has reached a critical mass. Our country's future is hanging in the balance, reliant on selfish, short-sighted demagogues.

The other arguments against term limits are all bogus. Being a senator or House member does not require a lot of training or experience. Good lawyers who become judges, which is a lot harder than being a legislator, don't need on-the-job training. As with good attorneys who become good trial and appellate judges, the quality of citizens-turned-legislators depends on the character, intelligence, prior experience, and temperament of the person, not on length of tenure in the new role. Committee positions and chairmanships don't have to be assigned by seniority. Assignments can be implemented based on competence and experience; and by secret voting by the members of the entire body. Another tiresome argument in favor of unlimited terms is that it takes a long time to develop a competent staff. Poppycock. Permanent members of senatorial and congressional staffs are as arrogant, corruptible, and self-interested as their masters. Junior members of such staffs turn over every term, regardless of whether their bosses remain in office.

If terms were limited to one, we would see a lot of new and almost certainly better talent replacing the present incumbents. A multitude of honest, competent, energetic, and successful men and women would line up to vie for their one term. They would not have to be rich, although some would be from prior business successes, and they would not be for sale. There are tens of thousands of bright, accomplished, and hardworking men and women out there who are not willing to do the lying, weaseling, and moneygrubbing required to get elected to Congress, who would step forward to participate in a one-term system. No one can seriously maintain that today's senators and representatives, with periodic exceptions, come from a high-level talent base or have a record of achievement. Too many have limited experience other than in politics, and too many remain in office only because of incumbency. Think of it this way. Elected federal politicians are our employees, and employers are entitled to insist on independent quality control. Low quality and failure are the results of lack of quality control.

Because of basic and immutable flaws in the human character, the many rewards that flow to long-term United States senators and representatives, as well as the myriad groups and individuals that buy and control them, it is no use trying to persuade legislators to vote less selfishly and more wisely. That will not happen, as long as elected public office is seen as a career instead of a temporary assignment.

CHAPTER 4

The American Left: its Control over Politicians

There has been an American Left since colonial times. Its origins and history are chronicled in Daniel J. Flynn's *A Conservative History of the American* Left, published in 2008 by Random House, Inc. Flynn wrote that the American Left has a history of ignoring or erasing its past failures and trumpeting its future and as yet unaccomplished triumphs. The American Left has only recently become a potent electoral force, with the money and will to exert heavy influence over a major political party. The American Left is organized and efficient, but is not any one identifiable organization. As I see it, its major components include labor unions; trial lawyers; environmentalists; a myriad of groups of community organizers that are both privately and government funded; the majority of newspapers and television networks; billionaires with their own agendas, like George Soros; the bulk of college and university academicians; and of course, the American Civil Liberties Union. The Left's relevance to *American Manifesto* is that it controls vast sums of money and uses that money both to help elect and then control the votes of United States senators and representatives. Federal legislators have in many cases become subservient to it. The positions that the Left requires those politicians to take are, in the opinions of many, against the best interests of America. We deserve better than a cadre of self-serving politicos who keep themselves in office by kowtowing to the likes of union bosses, rich lawyers, and George Soros, who funds MoveOn.org, Media Matters for America, and the Center for American Progress, all far-left organizations.[35]

The Left has opposed and undermined every American military action since World War II. Leaving aside whether the Korean Conflict and the Vietnam War were good or bad wars, the Left wanted us to lose each. It helped prevent a clear victory in Korea. It caused our demoralizing loss in Vietnam, not to mention the murder and torture of hundreds of thousands of South Vietnamese. It even ridiculed President Ronald Reagan's freeing our neighbor, Grenada, from despotic Marxist rule. It has consistently condemned our development and implementation of anti-missile defense, despite direct evidence that the former Soviet Union and now China and Iran want to be in a position to threaten us and control our behavior with land- and sea-based missiles. The Obama administration has reduced spending on strategic anti-missile defense in the face of clear threats of nuclear aggression by North Korea and Iran. In 2009 Defense Secretary Gates, with the approval of Obama, halted production of our next generation of fighter aircraft, the F-22, while Russia and China are busily developing their own advanced fighter aircraft and air defenses.[36] We have largely ceased maintaining our nuclear arsenal. The government even made public knowledge a matter that had been a state secret since World War II—the exact number of our nuclear warheads!

The Left's representatives in the Senate and House, while American soldiers were at daily risk in Iraq, loudly proclaimed that we were losing the war, until it became obvious that, despite their claims, we were winning. As I see it, a defining characteristic of the American Left since World War II has been to be quiet while the decision to fight is being made, and to oppose the war after we are committed to it by

---

35 John Gibson, *How the Left Swiftboated America* (New York: HarperCollins Publishers, 2009), 150.

36 Michael Auslin, "The Case for Reviving the F-22 Fighter," *The Wall Street Journal*, February 24, 2011.

undermining the war effort. It cannot be seriously argued that the incessant barrage of criticism of the Iraq War and those fighting it did not aid the enemy and place our soldiers at greater risk.

I also believe the Left is anti-business. To it, American industry—based on free enterprise, free markets, and the model of turning ideas, capital and labor into value—is at best questionable and at worst evil. The Left and its supporters on Capitol Hill want to increase the tax and regulatory burden on American business. One of its many legislative goals is the hallucinogenically[37] named Employee Free Choice Act, which would prevent employers from offering fair and legitimate opposition to labor union organizational campaigns. The Left, which includes major environmentalist groups, wants industry placed under a crippling regulatory burden on the strength of controversial and questionable science. The most successful plaintiffs' trial lawyers are, as a whole, allied with the Left. They oppose all efforts to curb their fee-producing assaults on American industry and the health-care system, and claim to have blocked any type of tort reform in the massive healthcare legislation narrowly passed in 2010.[38]

The American Left is enthusiastically and I contend hypocritically supportive of the interests of demanding racial minorities, illegal immigrants, and other people with no power other than the ability to vote. It supports redistribution of wealth from those who are best at earning it to those who earn less or nothing, without requiring any reciprocal effort from the recipients. It encourages affirmative action, a code name for race-based preferential treatment for minorities in employment and higher education. It supports teachers' labor unions and a failed government-operated education system that does not educate. It does all these things not because they do any good for the persons affected. It does them so that the affected persons will think

37 Peter A. List, a leading management consultant, gets credit for that colorful and accurate description.

38 Anthony Tarricone, President, American Association for Justice, f/k/a Association of Trial Lawyers of America, "AAJ's Healthcare Campaign in Review," letter to members, March 26, 2010.

something good is being done for them, and therefore they can be easily persuaded to vote for leftist candidates.

The American Left became identifiable in the early 1920s, following the 1917 Bolshevik Revolution in Russia and the founding of the Soviet Union. The Left became fascinated by the Soviet Union, Lenin, and Josef Stalin, a fascination that continues to this day. The American Left thinks Adolf Hitler was the only human monster of the twentieth century, not caring that Stalin and another of its heroes, Mao Tse-tung, each murdered many times more people than Hitler. Stalin's and Mao's respective tens of millions of murders occurred over decades, mainly during peacetime, and for Stalin's and Mao's political gain. Hitler's murders were far less in number, and while genocidal in nature, occurred almost entirely during a time of world war. That does not seem to matter. History as taught in American schools downplays the villainy of the Communist rulers and emphasizes that of Hitler. Ho Chi Minh was a murderous despot whose regime imprisoned, tortured, and murdered millions of Vietnamese before and during the wars fought by France and the United States in Vietnam. There is extensive documentation of that based on direct evidence.[39] Any number of other sources document Ho's countless murders—sometimes of entire villages—mutilations, and other politically and ideologically motivated atrocities. Regardless, Ho Chi Minh is a hero to the Left. The Left regards him, along with Stalin, Lenin, Mao, and other mass murderers, as "kindred spirits of the same faith."[40] Fidel Castro enjoys the same regard from the left.[41] To the Left, Che Guevara is a romantic revolutionary hero instead of a homicidal sociopath. College students to this day display his picture on dorm room walls and T-shirts. The Left's macabre delight in revolutionaries turned despots continues with its disregard of the ruinous plight of Zimbabwe under Robert Mugabe. To

39 "The Blood Red Hands of Ho Chi Minh," *Readers Digest*, November, 1968; Lam Thanh Liem, "Ho Chi Minh's Land Reform: Mistake or Crime?" *Su that ve Than and Su ngiep* (Paris: Nam A, 1990), pp. 200-205.

40 George Irbe, "Leftists," *George's Views* (blog), 1998, last modified March 7, 2001, accessed May 31, 2011, http://pages.interlog.com/~girbe/leftists.html.

41 Ibid.

the American Left, President George W. Bush deserved more scrutiny and opprobrium than any of the world's dictators, including those like Chavez of Venezuela, Mugabe of Zimbabwe, and Mahmoud Ahmadinejad of Iran, who despises America and openly proclaims his desire to wipe out Israel. Bush, at least, loves his country and spent two terms trying to make more countries and people around the world free. His efforts in that regard were met with skepticism, contempt, and hatred from the Left, and bitter criticism and impeachment threats from its agents in Congress.

The American Left is famous for its defense of Soviet spies and agents employed at high levels of the United States government before and during World War II, and for a decade after the war.[42] Long before the release and publication in 1995 of the Venona papers, the Left denied that the Departments of State, Commerce, Defense, and Justice, as well as other federal agencies, employed Soviet agents and others who were actively helping the Soviet Union. Based on evidence available during and immediately after World War II, let alone now, those denials are no more accurate than denials of the Holocaust. There can be fair debate about how many agents there were, how much damage they did, and some of the methods used to expose them, but no reasonable, unbiased historian denies that there were many of them. Much information (not value judgments, but factual information) on this is found in *Blacklisted by History* by M. Stanton Evans, and *Treason* by Ann Coulter. (Well, there may be a few value judgments in *Treason*.) *Blacklisted* is a history of Senator Joseph McCarthy's efforts to expose Soviet and Communist spies and agents who were government employees. *Treason* is a quick and entertaining must-read for anyone who wants to give consideration to whether past federal officials like Harry Truman, George C. Marshall, and Dean Acheson supported America or protected its enemies. And, regardless of what we have been programmed to think of McCarthy and his work, and regardless of the vicious attacks on Coulter (of whom the Left is deathly afraid), those

42 Ibid.

two books and their hundreds of sources offer well-documented and hard-to-dispute proof that many federal employees in high places used their government jobs to help the Soviets and hurt America. Prominent among them was Alger Hiss, who advised Franklin Roosevelt to accede to Soviet territorial demands at Yalta. There were American diplomat John Stewart Service and United States Treasury attaché Solomon Adler, who, with others, convinced President Truman to dump Chiang Kai-shek and endorse the Communist mass murderer, Mao, as ruler of China.[43] The "loss" of China to a murderous Communist despot was a foreign policy disaster, worse by far than Jimmy Carter's administration's enabling of anti-American Islamists to take over Iran. At least Carter did that on his own, with benign but misguided intentions. According to Evans and others, China was wrested from our World War II ally, Chiang, who owed us gratitude, and was given to our enemy, Mao, by American traitors whom Truman trusted and believed. China is now a main contender to replace us as the dominant world power.

The point here is not to recite history, although *Blacklisted* and *Treason* are worth reading exclusively for historical content, without regard to the opinions and judgments expressed in them. The point they make is that the American Left blindly, stubbornly, and angrily resisted all efforts to expose Communists and Soviet agents employed in our government from the 1930s to the 1950s. Alger Hiss was defended to the end by President Truman's Secretary of State, Dean Acheson. When Whittaker Chambers, the main witness against Hiss, presented his final and most conclusive evidence of Hiss's guilt, Truman wanted to indict Chambers for perjury![44] To this day, there are groups dedicated to reopening the Hiss case and exonerating him.

Another cause dear to some on the American Left is the Rosenberg case. Conclusive proof was presented that they had passed secret information about atomic weaponry to the Soviets, an act of treason that helped the Soviets become the other major nuclear power. An

43 M. Stanton Evans, *Blacklisted by History* (New York: Three Rivers Press, 2009), 105-106.

44 Evans, *Blacklisted*, 321-322.

oft-assumed reason for the treason of Julius and Ethel Rosenberg and their confederates was that the world would be a better place if military power between the United States and the Soviet Union were equalized.[45] (A case can be made that our current government is drifting in that direction, as evidenced by its cancellation of missile defenses in Eastern Europe, its indifference to the strength and secrecy of our nuclear arsenal, and the cancellation of our most advanced and effective fighter aircraft.) To this day, there are efforts to reopen the case and exonerate the Rosenbergs, who were executed in 1953.

The leftist attitudes of tolerance for, support for, and even loyalty to anti-American efforts and causes are prevalent today. In *Last Exit to Utopia*, a book by Jean-Francois Revel, subtitled *Survival of Socialism in a Post-Soviet Era*, Revel writes that one "can be a card-carrying member of the left with one simple qualification, well within the reach of anyone, however slow of mind: to be reflexively anti-American, at all costs and in all circumstances, whatever the event or the issue."[46] In these times, unlike in the cases discussed above, leftist attitudes and initiatives are backed by huge amounts of money, which is being offered and given to gullible and greedy United States senators and representatives. The persons and groups doing this, such as billionaires Peter B. Lewis and George Soros and Media Matters, headed by David Brock,[47] are not publicizing or explaining their rationale or efforts. An excellent source of detailed information on this is *The Shadow Party*, by David Horowitz and Richard Poe, published in 2006 by Nelson Communications, Inc. It explains how George Soros, through organizations funded by him and many others described as "sixties radicals," believes that the United States of America should cease being the leading world power. To that end, they urge that the American military be diminished, that America give huge sums of taxed money to the poor of the world, and

---

45 Louis Nizer, *The Implosion Conspiracy* (Garden City: Doubleday & Co., 1973).

46 Jean Francois Revel, *Last Exit to Utopia* (New York: Encounter Books, 2000), 8.

47 Michael Luo, "Left's Big Donors Gather to Plot Strategy," *New York Times*, November 15, 2010.

that American industry should be regulated as prescribed by radical environmental causes. Soros equated President Bush's unequivocal opposition to worldwide Islamic terrorism to Nazism.[48] Soros and various well-funded leftist organizations advocate that, instead of opposing terrorism with military force, we should tax ourselves and give the money to the terrorists, thus persuading them to end their violent practices. No group with a hidden agenda should have the opportunity to buy votes so as to advance such a scheme. Issues like that should be voted on by legislators who are unobligated.

Revel wrote in *Last Exit to Utopia* and an earlier book, *The Totalitarian Temptation*, published by Doubleday in 1977, that in every advanced society, including democratic ones, there is a "sizeable proportion of men and women who hate liberty – and consequently truth." Such people, wrote Revel, aspire "to live in a tyrannical system, whether as a participant in the exercise of power or, more strangely, as a slave to it." This, according to Revel, explains the "otherwise inexplicable rise and longevity of totalitarian regimes in countries that are among the most civilized on earth, such as Germany, Italy, China and Russia."[49] Another writer asserts that the Left has a "lust for domineering, coercive power over society," masked by a "proffered rationale" of "the interest of the common good."[50]

While my own opinions on these matters are not masked, the purpose here is not to discredit the American Left, but to identify it as one of the major influences on many federal politicians. Its contributions go to Democratic candidates. This explains why many members of that party in the Senate had to be shamed into expressing disapproval of MoveOn.org's full-page ad in the *New York Times*, referring to General David Petraeus as "General Betray Us," after he reported to Congress on our favorable progress in the Iraq War. Hillary Clinton, a close ally of Soros,[51] voted against the Senate resolution condemning the ad.

48 Horowitz and Poe, *The Shadow Party*, 15.

49 Revel, *Last Exit to Utopia*, 86.

50 Irbe, "Leftists," 1.

51 Horowitz and Poe, *The Shadow Party*, 53-64.

Senator Obama did not vote on that sensitive issue, as was characteristic of him while he was a state senator. Safer that way.

No group or groups with an agenda like that of the American Left should be given power over our foreign and domestic affairs. The Left's power on those important matters exists first and foremost because some senators and representatives apparently want to stay in office indefinitely. Remove that opportunity, and MoveOn.org, ACORN, Soros, labor unions, rich lawyers, environmental fanatics, the ACLU, and the organized American Left become no more than well-funded groups with opinions and the opportunities to express them. Limiting federal legislators to one term will mean that ideas, ideologies, and opinions, whether they are extreme or mainstream, stupid or brilliant, will be dealt with on their merits, and not on the basis of who offers money and other aid to incumbents. We, the American people, must control the resolution of the internal conflict described in chapter 1 by requiring that legislative decisions of great political, economic, military, and philosophical importance be decided on the basis of what is best for America, not what keeps selfish incumbents in power.

CHAPTER 5

A Free-Market Economy, or an American Brand of Socialism?

A major difference between a free-market economy and the sort of quasi-socialism favored by many members of Congress was offered by the late economist Milton Friedman. He said that "A major source of objection to a free economy is precisely that … it gives people what they want instead of what a particular group thinks they ought to want. Underlying most arguments against the free market is a lack of belief in freedom itself."[52] With that in mind, it appears to me that throughout history the strength or weakness of a nation's economy has determined its position in the world and the prosperity of its people. All over the world, free-market societies have succeeded and socialistic, government-controlled economies have failed. Apart from national defense, there is no more important area of decision making than our economy. Americans need legislators who are driven by wisdom and pragmatism instead of by the ideologies and the commands of their supporters and party bosses.

It is apparent to me that the American Left dislikes capitalism and distrusts American business. It claims that American industry is riddled with dishonesty, corruption, and criminal activity. It wants

52 Milton Friedman, "Constitutional Limitations on Government," accessed July 17, 2011, http://econfaculty.gmu.edu/wew/ quotes/govt.html.

government to control business with increasingly intrusive regulation. At the same time, it supports labor unions, which in too many cases really are infested with corruption and criminal activity. What business corporation can you name that admitted in a judicial consent decree, as the International Brotherhood of Teamsters did in 1989, to being dominated by four crime families? For that reason, the Teamsters are under federal supervision to this day.

The American Left also thinks the federal government should take more money in taxes from the most successful and productive businesses. It helped bring about the government takeovers of General Motors and Chrysler Corporation. It is behind the push for federal control of health care, at our expense. As reported on WorldNetDaily.com, a couple of leftist members of Congress, California's Maxine Waters and Maurice Hinchey of New York, stated in 2008 that the government should nationalize the major United States oil companies.[53] Some Democrats wanted to impose a windfall profits tax on the oil companies that we depend on to meet our energy needs. Secretary of State Hillary Clinton suggested this when she was a senator. These officials ignore and obscure the fact that the oil companies' profit margins—that is, their percentage of return on capital—is the same as or lower than American industry as a whole. They seem not to care whether those vital businesses (with hundreds of thousands of employees) succeed or fail. The Left either does not understand or does not care how the actions it advocates will affect the American economy.

A major failure of President George W. Bush is that when he could have, he did nothing to curtail the profligate and incurable spending habits of Congress. Senators and representatives are addicted to spending our money like the worst alcoholic is addicted to drink, and so was Bush. Presidential veto power is meant to control congressional excesses in spending and other ill-advised legislative action. Many people who supported Bush felt betrayed because he failed to prevent

53 "Dems Want Control over U.S. Oil Flow, Hinchey Joins Waters, Says 'We should own refineries,'" June 18, 2008, accessed November 5, 2010, http://www.wnd.com/?pageId=674.90.

the truly remarkable amount of outrageous congressional spending during his tenure.

Apart from that costly failure, in 2008 Bush and Senator John McCain had a different economic plan than the Democrats. Republicans have confidence in American business and the ability of American businesspeople to maintain and expand our economy. Republicans, especially those who have owned or operated businesses, believe that economic success is based on incentive-driven behavior, and that businesspeople succeed because they think their hard work and risk will be rewarded. They maintain that wealth and value are created by private sector businesses, and that anyone who is willing to work hard is entitled to a chance to become wealthier than those who do not work hard.

However, too many federal lawmakers demonstrate no better understanding of basic business principles than did the planners of the failed Soviet economy. They assume that American business will always rise to the occasion, that the economy will always be strong, and that new value will always be created. In turn, more money will be earned, from which more taxes can be taken. They apparently don't understand or don't care who generates the tax base that makes federal spending possible. They don't care that the top 1 percent of American money earners are already paying 38 percent of the tax burden, while the bottom 50 percent are bearing 2.7 percent of that burden.[54] Nor that about 45 percent of households pay no income tax at all![55] The "rich," (those earning over $159,000), are taxed far more heavily than others, paying nearly 60 percent of federal income taxes, despite their share of aggregate income being 35 percent.[56] Those who urge even higher taxes on those high earners are unconcerned with how much more of that treatment the successful and productive people in this country are willing to take. Federal legislators who wish to further

54 John Merline, "Rich Pay Growing Share of Tax," *Investor's Business Daily*, April 27, 2011.

55 Ibid.

56 Ibid.

burden successful people and successful businesses with higher taxes cannot have understood *Atlas Shrugged* by Ayn Rand.[57] In Rand's novel, successful and productive people got tired of socialism, dropped out, withheld their creativity and productivity from the fictional parasitic United States government, and formed their own exclusive and prosperous society.

The American Left has little good to say about business or industry. Part of its position on the economy has to do with giving labor unions more power over employers and workers. It apparently ignores the fact that American workers and American employers, operating in harmony and without unions, have been the most successful economic dream team the world has ever known. As John Kerry did in 2004, Barack Obama in 2008 sought to set American workers against the businesses that employ them. He also wants to raise income taxes and capital gains taxes on the most successful and productive of us and place special taxes on certain essential industries, such as health insurance, energy, and banking. Obama and many in Congress are demonizing these industries so as to mislead us into thinking they deserve punishment. Each new and higher tax means more power for the federal government. Sound familiar? You read about it in *The Communist Manifesto*, in which Karl Marx wrote that the progressive income tax is a primary instrument in the destruction of a democracy.

The vitality of American business determines the state of the economy. Some Republicans and a few Democrats understand that, and therefore do not demonize business. Think back to the years following the American Revolution. After our military victory, the first thing we had to do to survive was to get an economy going, which we initially did by borrowing from the Netherlands and others. The United States, like all other civilizations for over six millennia, is a money-based society. Goods and services are traded for money. Most members of society are motivated by acquiring enough money to live on, and then they often seek to acquire more than is necessary for survival. Since the

57 Ayn Rand, *Atlas Shrugged* (New York: Random House, Inc., 1957).

beginning of modern civilization, that has been an axiom of human behavior.

Federal legislators don't pay attention to that, unless it involves their own fortunes. You never hear them say that the money the government receives from taxes is our money. They see it as the government's money, or *their* money. They malign successful people for wanting to keep a little more of what they earn, instead of having it taken in taxes. The government desires to control such people by imposing even higher tax rates on them. Some legislators accused President Bush and Vice President Cheney of having had illicit relationships with "big business" without offering a scintilla of proof. Bush had a realistic grasp of human behavior insofar as money and economic achievement are concerned. He knew that of the more than three hundred million people in this country, the relatively modest number who create, maintain, and expand successful businesses are those who are mainly responsible for creating and producing value and wealth. (This is not to downplay the essential role of the American worker. The American dream couldn't happen without his and her dedicated efforts.) But someone has to get the businesses off the ground. Without the large variety of successful and profitable businesses this country produces, America would collapse. If such businesses and their creators are discouraged by being forced to pay higher marginal tax rates that are applied only to them, America will sag. Only the private business sector produces wealth and value. Government does not produce either; it only takes them.

What won the American Civil War? It wasn't that the Union soldiers were more courageous or skillful, but rather that the Union's superior economy and means of production wore down the South. Another example is World War II. Our men and women in arms were courageous, but the war was largely won by the ability of our industry-based economy, between January 1942 and December 1943, to produce war materiel such as the world had never seen. American industry had to do that before our fighting people could succeed in battle. A lot of businesses and people earned money in the process, bought good and services, and paid taxes on their profits.

In the same way, the contemporary American businessperson has to start, grow, and guide a business so that the American worker can have employment. All of the Americans who are involved in American business activity, regardless of their level or role, need to succeed, create new value, and earn money in order for tax revenue to be available for federal, state, and local treasuries. No one does that because they have to, but because they are seeking economic success and a better standard of living.

Republicans tend to propose letting successful and productive individuals keep more of what they earn. They have a positive attitude toward business (so long as it behaves itself). Big business, big oil, big manufacturing, big pharmaceuticals, big whatever, all of them are an essential part of what makes America great. The GOP understands that, and it understands that excessive regulation and retaliatory taxation are destructive. It understands that those are major reasons why American businesses maintain operations and workforces in other countries. It also understands that as the inexorable upward march of human population continues, there will be unavoidable blows to the environment. They avoid demagoguery about flawed fads, like the Kyoto Protocol, not to mention Cap and Trade, either of which would place disabling and discriminatory burdens on American industry, while giving powerful nations like China and India a free pass to continue polluting.

Republicans also understand that small businesses, which employ anywhere from four or five people to one thousand employees, are often family owned and are a major part of the American economy. The main reason Bush proposed abolition of the federal estate tax was so that individuals would feel free to establish small businesses and spend their lives expanding them, with the knowledge that upon their deaths, their heirs would not have to close the business, fire the workers, sell the assets, and pay 55 percent of the proceeds to the government.

In 2004, John Kerry and John Edwards talked about "Two Americas," trying to sell the notion that there is an undeserving, overprivileged class of rich people; a shrinking middle class; an unhappy and struggling working class; and a large group of deserving but poverty-stricken individuals. That notion is not just misleading, it's downright false. Look at who made that up—Edwards, a wealthy trial lawyer, who looted hospitals and physicians by spouting now-discredited science to gullible juries. In 2004, Bush won South Carolina, Edwards's home state, and North Carolina, where Edwards was a first-term senator. What does that say? Anyone who knows about the mansions that John Edwards, as well as the Obamas, the Clintons, the Gores, Nancy Pelosi, the Kennedys, and others live in, understands which America they inhabit.

There are wealthy, undeserving, and overprivileged groups in America. One, in my opinion, is the so-called Hollywood elites. They receive huge sums of money but produce nothing of tangible value. They are worshipped as celebrities, and therefore have an audience for their rantings about the evils of American values. The plaintiffs' trial lawyers who contribute so heavily to Democrats are also hugely rich, yet they also produce nothing—they just transfer money from defendants to their clients and themselves. But those groups are not targeted in the attacks politicians level at whom they call "the wealthy." Instead, senators and representatives vilify and demonize the people who create and operate major businesses, as well as oil companies, manufacturing companies, banks, and large agricultural enterprises along with the people who start and operate successful small businesses, contractors, subcontractors, small manufacturers, and retailers. Business owners, large and small, take the risk, put up the money, suffer losses when things go wrong, and make the products and services we buy. They create the jobs that boost the economy. They, not entertainers, lawyers, and politicians, create real and lasting value, including millions of jobs, yet they are criticized and penalized by the Left and its political servants. Successful entrepreneurs are viewed with distrust, suspicion, and, in some cases, hostility by the Reid-Pelosi crowd. Conservative politicians view them with optimism and offer them encouragement.

During the 2008 campaign, the Democrats promised new government programs. One is a system of national health care. They promised that everyone, whether they could pay for it or not, would have health insurance. Numerous economists have attempted to quantify the cost of this. The reliable figures are in the trillions of dollars. The plan, which passed in 2010 and which I discuss in chapter 13, features government control of the health-care choices we now make for ourselves.

What is wrong with all of this? Leaving aside my own views on the outcome of these issues, what is wrong—but correctible—is that the majorities in Congress are making crucial legislative decisions largely based on self-interest. Those decisions are favored by those who got those legislators elected, while the well-being of America is disregarded. What the party bosses and their minions are forcing on us may doom our economy and harm our already fragile culture. It has much, of course, to do with pleasing and buying the votes of the multitudes of Americans who pay no income taxes. All those Americans have a vote, and they are told that the rich should pay higher taxes. Indeed, polls indicate that the public favors raising taxes on wealthier taxpayers.[58]

Tax increases, however, always lower the overall tax base. Tax rate reductions expand it. Research has shown that since the 1920s, during the Coolidge years, across-the-board tax rate cuts caused *higher* tax payments and a *larger* share of tax paid by high earners. That also happened as the result of lower tax rates initiated by Presidents Kennedy and Reagan.[59] Christina Romer, who was the director of Obama's Council of Economic Advisers until she apparently said the wrong thing, stated: "Tax changes have very large effects on output. Our [research] suggests that an exogenous tax increase of 1% of GDP lowers real GDP by roughly 3%."[60] How can that be? Simple. High achievers in business change their business behavior in accordance with tax rates, since all people—the rich, liberals, conservatives, and

58 John Merline, "Rich Pay Growing Share of Tax," *Investor's Business Daily*, April 27, 2011.

59 "Cal vs. Krug," *Investor's Business Daily*, April 12, 2011.

60 Rep. Paul Ryan, "Four Pro-Growth Axioms to Avert Shared Scarcity," *Investor's Business Daily*, May 17, 2011.

libertarians—try to avoid taxes.[61] The proof of that is that since 1960, federal tax collections have been between 15 percent and 20 percent of GDP every year; yet during the same period, the top marginal tax rate has been between 91 percent and 35 percent.[62] Thus, whether tax rates are high or low, people and businesses adjust their economic behavior so that the government's take stays the same. "Differences in tax rates have a far greater impact on economic growth than [on] federal revenues."[63] Otherwise put by a professor of economics at Stanford University, "as college students learn in Econ 101, higher marginal tax rates cause real economic harm" because higher tax rates negatively influence business incentives, and "as tax rates rise, the tax base shrinks."[64]

Nonetheless, the Democrats have not said much about cutting federal spending and a lot about raising taxes. Between January and July 2009, the Democratic-controlled House and Senate committed to spend trillions of dollars we do not have, and which future generations will have to somehow earn to pay back. That was in keeping with campaign promises that lawmakers seeking further terms made during the 2008 election season.

If that is not bad enough, a noneconomic problem with their actions, including government-controlled health care, is that it encourages behavior that has become too common in America, and is harming the character and culture of the American people. Self-reliance built America; reliance on government to cure one's health, financial, and other problems may destroy it. Many people have written over many years that the greatest risk for a democracy is that voters will learn that they can reach into the pockets of others and vote themselves money earned by others. Benjamin Franklin is thought to have said "When the people find out that they can vote themselves money, that will herald the end of the Republic." When it is possible to remain

61 Walter Williams, "Tax the Rich? Good Luck with That," *Investor's Business Daily*, April 12, 2011.

62 Ibid.

63 Ibid.

64 Michael J. Boskins, "Get Ready for a 70% Marginal Tax Rate," *Wall Street Journal*, July 18, 2011.

idle, keep having babies, and receive money to live on without earning it, there are many who cannot resist. That conduct is a blight on our national character, and it is encouraged by vote-buying by lawmakers using *our* money.

From the beginning, our greatness has been based on the individual relying on him or herself for well-being, success, and happiness. When the United States was formed, the European countries were dominated by hereditary aristocracies. In America, we attain status by succeeding at something useful, thereby achieving recognition and wealth. It's natural for people who earn more money than the average individual to be able to afford better medical care, along with better legal representation and a lot of other things. That's why we strive for success. It's not a sin to be successful and become wealthy, and to live accordingly. It is interesting how leftist politicians, the Hollywood elites, and the trial lawyers tell the American people that big business and the wealthy are wrongdoers, and they need to be regulated, punished, and stripped of their wealth through tax increases and litigation. Anyone who has read about John Edwards's tax avoidance devices, as described in a 2004 *Wall Street Journal* article, will know how hypocritical Edwards was on that issue. The tax shelters used by the Kennedys are well known. No one is heartless enough to advocate doing away with all subsidization of the truly needy, but the coerced transfers of wealth from those who have worked for their money to those who don't have gone too far and are not helping our nation or its people.

An annoying thing about the Left is its incessant mantra about "tax cuts for the wealthy." Anyone who understands federal income taxation knows that one result of Bush's tax relief was an increased number of truly poor people who pay no income taxes. Everybody who pays taxes had their taxes reduced; the rate reductions were across the board. The Left and its minions in Congress call the successful individuals who create and expand business activity and employment opportunities and thereby achieve higher earnings the "wealthy" and the "rich" in hopes of being seen as the champions of the lower earners. The characterization of Bush's marginal rate reductions as "tax cuts for the wealthy" is misleading and self-serving. The only grain of truth is that the "wealthy" (the successful, the hard-working, the producers) received the largest tax reductions in gross dollars because they always were—and still are—paying the most in taxes.

The Left also lied about why Bush proposed tax rate reduction. *There is not one shred of evidence that it was done to please any particular person, business, or interest group.* The reason Bush proposed tax relief was to give incentive to people to work harder and smarter, especially those who were most responsible for making the economy grow. In contrast, every major piece of legislation passed since 2009 involves new spending, which will require major tax hikes.

Since the inception of our country, our economy has been the opposite of a state-planned economy. We saw from the failure of the Soviet Union how badly that works. Note how Cuba's state-run economy has kept that country in abject poverty for years, and how Hugo Chavez and his socialistic measures have turned Venezuela into an economic train wreck. America's economy is based on the entrepreneurial spirit and reward-driven human behavior. A person has an idea. He or she has or borrows money, places it at risk, hires and pays others, and makes a product or presents a service. If the product or service is good enough, people buy it, and the entrepreneur and the employees make money. Such men and women need an incentive to do more of that, and on a bigger scale. Bush's rationale was that if you allow successful and productive people to keep a little more of the money they earn, they will create more business activity, hire more employees, produce more value, and thereby expand the base from which all taxes are generated. From the evidence, Bush's tax rate reductions created enormous economic growth from 2002-2007. It is a matter of record that greatly increased tax revenues followed those rate cuts.

In the opinion of many, the financial crisis of 2007-2009 was caused first and foremost by federal government interference with private lending and credit markets. A recent book co-written by a *New York Times* business writer asserts that the problem began with the Clinton administration's obsession with more people of less-than-modest means owning homes. Lenders, urged on by Fannie Mae and Freddie Mac, abandoned long-held real estate lending standards.[65] That ultimately led to a worldwide market for securities that were backed by uncollectible mortgage loans that should never have been made. Representative Barney Frank and former Senator Chris Dodd, who are in the front row of responsibility for the disastrous government meddling, have denied their culpability, even in the face of hard-to-dispute evidence that inculpates them. Both chambers of Congress took advantage of the crisis to pass legislation designed to take money earned by successful businesses and businesspeople and redistribute it through new or expanded government programs. In my opinion, those programs, like all such initiatives since Lyndon Johnson's Great Society, will not do any lasting good, will maintain a class of people that is dependent on government, and will do great damage to the private sector economy.

The law firm of which I am a partner proved how lower tax rates create value. About 450 people work at our firm. The lower marginal tax rates prompted us to work harder. More importantly, they caused our business clientele to do more business, and thereby need more legal work. The greatest expansion of our firm and its practice, and our greatest success, came in the 2001-2007 period. Our experience was a small model, replicated all over America. The results meant more individuals received more personal income on which federal income taxes were paid. It meant more homes were bought on which the owners paid local taxes; and more goods were bought, from which the state received sales taxes. It was the ever-valid example of the real-value pie getting bigger, and everyone who shared the pie receiving benefit. It shouldn't take an economist to know that energizing and increasing the tax base is a much better way of putting money in the federal treasury, not to mention state and local treasuries, than increasing already high taxes on successful and productive people.

The argument should have been settled by an essay in the *Wall*

65 Gretchen Morgenson and Joshua Rosner, *Reckless Endangerment* (New York: Times Books/Henry Holt & Company, 2011).

Street Journal in 2004 by R. Glenn Hubbard, dean of the Columbia University Business School. Dean Hubbard wrote that tax cuts have a "potent effect" on "willingness to assume the risk of a new venture and to hire additional workers", and that Senator Kerry's proposal to "raise income tax rates substantially on higher-income individuals would throw the job machine into reverse, with adverse implications for business formation and employment." That, from an Ivy League academician! And he was right. The Bush tax rate reductions resulted in a monumental increase in aggregate federal taxes collected. Too bad he allowed Congress to waste much of it on vote-buying schemes.

The entrenched federal legislators do not want to hear about tax reductions creating new value and expanding the tax base. They want to talk about how the wealthy are increasing the gap between themselves and the poor, are wiping out the middle class, are oppressing the poor and minorities, and therefore should be punished. They refuse to use language other than the "wealthy" or the "rich," although they know that the people they are maligning are, in fact, the successful and productive. They engage in this self-serving sophistry because voters tend to believe it and vote accordingly.

One of the *really* rich is Senator John Kerry, who has the benefit of his wife's vast fortune, which she inherited from her late husband, John Heinz, a Republican United States Senator. Another is Edwards, who made millions suing doctors and hospitals (including nonprofit ones). Hillary Clinton and her husband are worth over one hundred million dollars, earned entirely by writing books, giving speeches, and doing favors, all because of their government-bestowed celebrity status. Obama and his wife are multimillionaires, thanks to two autobiographies he wrote, which people bought after he became a celebrity. But the Left (and the media) adore such people; they are not the targeted "rich" and "wealthy."

What does all this have to do with elected politicians and reelection? It is partly that a majority of senators and representatives are influenced by groups that favor more government control over business as well as over successful businesspeople. A good way to control the latter, as Karl

Marx wrote, is by taking more of their earnings. Following the Marxist rationale, our federal legislators want to control more and more of the value created by our high achievers. But it is also because the lawmakers are hoping to buy the support of the nonachievers.

To the latter end, our lawmakers encourage class warfare between the poor and rich (the unsuccessful and the successful), and carry on the drumbeat of minority victimhood, also known as race-baiting. Leftist politicians encourage individuals with lower incomes to believe that they are victims, that they are poor for reasons other than their own choices. Capitalism, they say, is to blame. The poor, these politicians say, should vote for them so they can take money from the wealthy and spend it to benefit the poor. The Left wants a permanent, victim-minded underclass that it can use to keep its candidates in office. This massive, cynical vote-buying scheme is one of the most blameworthy things elected politicians do. By promising higher taxes on successful men and women, and greater spending for the alleged benefit of less successful and less productive individuals, the politicians are buying their next terms with *our* money. In the process, they are willing to wreck our economy. They are also perpetuating the kind of behavior that causes people, business organizations, and countries to fail. It is no accident that so many young people drop out of school, become dependent on drugs, have children out of wedlock whom they cannot support, and resist hard work. They are being encouraged in all those directions by politicians who want to buy their votes. Voters, before falling for that siren song and selling their votes, must understand that if they depend on money and benefits given by another, they must be satisfied with whatever the donor chooses to give. In such a system, the donor (the government) is the ruler, and the recipients are the subjects.

Successful, well-paid, happy, and positive-thinking individuals don't sell their votes, and they do not vote for politicians who want to rule them. Honest, altruistic politicians would *want* more successful, happy, well-paid, and positive-thinking people in the electorate. Legislators limited to one term would not care who those people voted for in the next election, because they would not be running. Placing the single-term limit on all elected federal politicians would set the stage for an honest choice between a free-market economy and an American brand of socialism. In my opinion, the resulting legislation would revitalize our economy and would be a giant step toward the personal accountability, self-reliance, and excellence that built our nation.

CHAPTER 6

Relations between Nations are Not about Friendship

In this chapter and the others on foreign and military policy, I acknowledge the role of presidents. Federal lawmakers, however, have major influence in such matters, not only because they control the money, but also because of what they say. Accordingly, two dangerous malfeasances of federal legislators are their pandering to voters who are tired of war and who do not understand why we need a strong military and why we need to fight on occasion; and their slavelike obedience to well-funded leftist groups like MoveOn.org, which in my opinion want America to avoid or lose wars. If left unchecked, I believe entrenched senators and representatives who are obligated to leftists may preside over our destruction. I envision the Left-controlled federal legislators would be the first to surrender to and collaborate with conquering forces.

Relatively few Americans know much about war. Those who know of it from experience don't like talking about it. When our armed forces go into combat and the engagement lasts a while, and troops are maimed and killed, the public comes to see the hardships as more important than the objective. Many lawmakers who vote for the military action later turn or are turned against it. Many congresspeople who supported and voted for the Iraq War became vocal opponents of it. This happened when it seemed to them that a majority of Americans were tired of the Iraq War and that they could do political damage to George W. Bush. Then they became vocal critics of the war and advocates of failure and defeat. It is my opinion that the politicians who publicly attacked the war in the midst of the fighting did so partly to gain political favor by discrediting President Bush, and partly in hopes of getting financial support from far-left antiwar groups. Regardless of their motives, the federal lawmakers who commit these vote-buying and support-seeking acts by changing their official positions during wartime to suit voters or monied interests are a menace to America. They either don't know, or perhaps don't care, how relations between sovereign nations work and how power and the credible threat of force play a crucial role.

Any rational individual would prefer to talk his way out of a potentially dangerous situation rather than fight. Even among people, however, at times that is not possible. Talking is how humans communicate with each other. Talking and offering to give something of value is one way in which we persuade others to do things for our benefit. That is called negotiation. However, in order to persuade another to alter a course of action on a matter of real importance, a credible threat of force or an act of force can be necessary. In dealings between individuals, the force or threat thereof is usually of a legal nature, but the ultimate potential force is violence or physical restraint. Imagine how unprincipled and aggressive people would act, and how we would fare, if we did not have laws, police forces, courts, and prisons.

Among nations, however, mere talk on matters of great importance is usually worthless, other than as a communication tool. Nations do not compromise their interests without good reason. Offering a sovereign nation benefits in exchange for action or inaction is expensive, and can result in the payer being lied to and cheated. The only way to effectively persuade a sovereign nation to change its behavior on a matter of importance, in which its preferred behavior threatens others, is by a persistent and credible threat of force. Such force may be partly of an economic nature, but history has shown that economic measures that are not backed up with a believable military threat are without value.

The Left accused President George W. Bush of damaging America's international friendships and alliances. Apparently for the Left, it is impermissible for the United States to advance or defend its interests by unilateral action, especially of a military nature. The American Left claims that the United States should not take controversial actions that affect other countries without agreement from "our allies." It is unclear who these allies are. During George W. Bush's two terms, many federal lawmakers urged that the United States' international relations should be practiced by international committee. Powerful elements of the American Left, including the organizations controlled or funded by Soros, advocate that the United States should not be the supreme world power, and that it should allow a consensus among so-called allied nations to control its major decisions on military action.

The view that the United States should obtain permission from other nations before taking action in its national interest defies the first and most important axiom of international relations: sovereign nations, when they have the power to do so, always act in their own interests, without regard to the interests of other nations. A corollary to that is that they either conceal their intentions, or lie about them. For example, we allowed North Korea to dupe us into giving it billions of dollars in aid, in exchange for a promise to cease its nuclear weapons program. North Korea almost immediately broke that promise, and its atomic weapons program is now a reality and a major problem for us. Lying among individuals is seen as immoral. Fraud (causing a person or business to give or relinquish something of value by material misrepresentation) gets you sued. But among nations, lying and its companion, nondisclosure, are simply tools to serve the national interest.

Several thousand years before Christ was born, humans began organizing into nations. The concept of a nation is engrained in the human psyche, and is here to stay. Ancient Greece, Rome, and the Byzantine Empire are early examples of advanced and powerful nations.

Over the centuries, some nations were more powerful than others, some had more advanced civilizations, and some were more primitive. Over the centuries all of those ancient civilizations had one thing in common: they were invaded, conquered, and in many cases enslaved by or annihilated by ruthless enemies who were more militarily powerful and whose soldiers were more willing to die to get what they wanted.

The examples are endless. The Greeks and other advanced civilizations fell to Rome. After Rome fell to barbarians, part of the Roman Empire became the Byzantine Empire, based in Constantinople (now Istanbul). The Ottoman Turks conquered that empire and ruled that part of the world, because they were militarily powerful and ruthless.

In more recent centuries, the major players were European nations. Spain and Portugal had their turns. At one point, Spain was conquered by Arabs, because the Arabs were aggressive and more powerful. In the 1600s and early 1700s, France was a dominant nation. The eighteenth century saw a struggle play out between the French and British. The British won, in part due to a larger and more powerful navy, and in part to not having been divided and drained by a bloody and costly revolution. Our own country won independence not only through military force and sacrifices, but because French military power tipped matters in our favor at a critical time. In the years leading up to World War I, we had become one of several major nations in the world. Our military power tipped the balance in that war. During World War II, France, China, and many others nations were conquered and occupied by more aggressive and powerful nations. Prior to the war, England and France had wrung their hands and engaged in self-delusion while Nazi Germany built up its forces, preparing for what became a ghastly and completely avoidable world war. By the end of World War II, we were the dominant nation in the world, thanks to our military power. The Soviet Union was our main rival until the 1990s, thanks to our healthy respect for its nuclear arsenal and our uncertainty as to whether it would use it.

There will always be dominant nations in the world whose citizens therefore have better lives (or the opportunity for better lives). That cannot happen, in the final analysis, without the credible threat of effective military force, and its use when necessary. It is axiomatic that in human affairs, that condition is unavoidable.

Thanks in part to Americans who saw Stalin and the Soviet Union as friendly comrades-in-arms instead of as ruthless, self-interested conquerors, the United States allowed the Soviet Union to take control of Eastern Europe at the end of World War II. That happened despite public knowledge that the Soviet Union had repressed, tortured, and murdered a lot of more humans than had Nazi Germany. For the next five and a half decades of what came to be called the Cold War, we lived in fear of nuclear annihilation. No one except partisan leftists believes that Ronald Reagan didn't win the Cold War with his outspoken and aggressive attitude toward the Soviet Union and his revitalization of our armed forces. In 1986, when Reagan walked out on Gorbachev at the summit conference in Iceland, refusing (to the horror of leftists and the *New York Times*) to back off from the Strategic Defense Initiative, the Soviet Union was defeated. It just took a few more years for it and everyone else to realize that. What made that possible? Part of it was Reagan's attitude, which revived the American spirit that had become so demoralized following Vietnam and Jimmy Carter's presidency. The main variable, however, was the superior American free-market economy and the renewal of our military power, which had declined after Vietnam. The critical point that the American Left either ignores or does not care about is that some nations will be dominant, some will not, and that no rational person would rather live in a nation that is not. No intellectually honest American would prefer to live with the fear we had of the Soviets from 1950 until the Reagan years, let alone with the real threat we faced. And no honest person can dispute that the reason we do not live in fear is that we got stronger and they got weaker. As Reagan famously said, "We win, they lose"; and he made us economically and militarily strong enough to make that happen.

Another unvarying rule is that uncoerced nations cooperate with one another only in limited ways, and only when and for as long as it suits their national interests. Otherwise, when they have the power to do so, they act in their own interest. In recent history, Hitler's Germany and Stalin's Soviet Union became allies in 1939, until Hitler decided in 1941 that it was in Germany's interest to betray and attack the Soviets. Germany and Japan were allies of convenience during World War II, and initiated the most destructive war in human history against countries with which they are now allied. Britain and France had a mutual assistance treaty in the late 1930s, which is why Britain got into the war when France was attacked. Yet during the preceding centuries, Britain and France had fought each other many times, killing millions, in their battle for dominance over each other. They certainly weren't allies then; they were bitter enemies. They did terrible things to each other to further their goals, such as England's expulsion of the French-leaning Acadians from Nova Scotia in 1755, due to perceived disloyalty. France and England became allies prior to the First World War because it was in their interest to combine against a more powerful Germany. The national interest of each separate nation is the *only* thing that can create an alliance and determine how strong or weak the alliance is and how long it lasts.

The United States of America is the primary nation that sacrifices significant amounts of money and effort, including human lives, to help other nations that do not always reciprocate. We are also the only major world power that thinks it is in our interest to fight for the freedom of others. A case can be made that we could have sat out World War II and let the Russians, Germans, and other combatants wear one another out. No one has ever seriously claimed that the Germans could have conquered us, although after their easy conquest of France, they could have taken Britain. But for the Pearl Harbor attack by Japan, we might have stayed out of it. That attack caused an overnight swing in public and congressional opinion, to the view that joining the fight was in our national interest. Before that, there was, as there is now, a dedicated and widely followed antiwar and isolationist view in our country. The Lend-Lease Act, which provided unused American shipping capacity to England in 1940—and probably saved England—passed Congress by one vote! Part of that was because citizens just did not want a war. After the Pearl Harbor attack, a strong sentiment developed in this country to help our supposed European allies, which included Stalin's Soviet Union, out of their difficulties. Our industrial strength and our newly-acquired will to fight saved much of the free world.

Prior to the 2004 and 2008 elections, Democrats and some Republicans could not stop talking about how they would restore our alliances after their alleged destruction during the years Bush was in office. What alliances? The closest thing we have to a true ally is Great Britain. It was in our interest to save Great Britain in 1941, and the British gave us important support after September 11, 2001. But go back to 1776 and envision the horrible fates the British, in the name of their national interest, would have inflicted on our founding fathers (and some mothers) if we had lost the fight. France? Give me a break. The last time France did anything for us was during our Revolutionary War, when it helped us for the sole purpose of harming England. Charles DeGaulle, the leader of the French Resistance in World War II, began trashing us soon after he became president of France. France was conquered in six weeks by Germany in 1940 and became a non-combatant puppet of the Germans until Allied military force liberated it in 1944. French collaboration with the Nazis during those years is a matter of record. Since World War II, France has frequently acted in its own interests anytime it wanted to. France has been one factor in keeping us from taking effective measures against Iran's nuclear weapons program. In Germany's case, from the end of World War II until 1990, there were two nations, one a western democracy created by the Allies, and one a communist state created by the Soviets. Germany also acts in its own interests, which means that it often disagrees with us.

France and Germany are two of the countries leftists refer to when they talk about how Bush destroyed our alliances. France and Germany were mortal enemies of each other from the 1870s through 1945. Our enemy in the Cold War, the Soviet Union, became an ally of sorts in World War II purely because we were on the same side against

Germany. A dying president, Franklin Roosevelt, and his advisors—which included Alger Hiss, a proven Soviet agent—allowed the Soviet Union to gobble up an unequal share of the spoils after World War II. I refer to Poland, Czechoslovakia, Hungary, Rumania, Bulgaria, Latvia, and Lithuania. Ronald Reagan would have dispatched General Douglas MacArthur with a suitable military force to send the Red Army back where it belonged, east of Ukraine. The use of atomic bombs might or might not have been mentioned, and the implicit threat would have worked. At that time Stalin, like Hitler in 1937, would have had no choice but to comply. How different post-1945 history would be! All of those important events in recent world history were unilateral actions taken by nations acting in their own interests and using either the believable threat of force or force.

Many lawmakers were hysterically critical of George W. Bush, but were silent on what they would have done to get France, Germany, Russia, or anyone else to act in our national interest instead of their own. That's because the answer is nothing. Those countries didn't oppose the Iraq War because Bush wasn't cosmopolitan, articulate, or diplomatic enough. They probably opposed it largely because they and Saddam Hussein were business partners. One may wonder why many former Soviet bloc countries helped us in the Iraq War. In my opinion, their experience with living under Soviet rule after WWII and their appreciation of the Reagan/United States Cold War victory which freed them made them want to be on a winning team that favors freedom over oppression. Now, as a result of our decommitment from placing antimissile defenses in Poland and the Czech Republic, one wonders if they would help us now.

Russia and China are obstructing our so-far-fruitless efforts to stop Iran from becoming a nuclear power because it is in their national interest to do so. We are relying on talk and ineffective sanctions instead of military force.[66] In my opinion, the only thing that will prevent Iran from having nuclear weapons is military force.

66 "So Long, Sanctions," *Investor's Business Daily*, May 24, 2010.

What and who are politicians talking about when they say America should act in accordance with other nations, instead of unilaterally? They are talking about our friend the United Nations, that's who. The United Nations that allowed the wholesale mutilation and slaughter of eight hundred thousand souls in Rwanda and withdrew its peacekeeping force when the going got tough. Yes, that's the same United Nations that allowed the worst genocide in Europe since World War II, before a NATO force led by the United States finally ended it. I refer to the United Nations troops in the "safe haven" of Srebrenica, who stood by while Serbian officers and soldiers assembled thousands of Muslim men for slaughter. It's also the same United Nations that allowed the United States to be kicked off its Human Rights Commission, and two years later elected that benign, humanitarian state, Sudan, to sit on the commission. The United Nations waffled and delayed while Arab militias in the Darfur region of Sudan murdered, mutilated, raped, and displaced tens of thousands of helpless Africans without provocation. One memorable United Nations contribution was former Secretary-General Kofi Annan's unilateral declaration that our liberation of Iraq from Saddam Hussein was "illegal." That was after *seventeen* United Nations resolutions had demanded Iraq's compliance with 1991 cease-fire conditions, and was just what Iraq needed leading up to free elections in Iraq. Another United Nations initiative was sending a representative to tour the United States, like a modern Alexis de Tocqueville, to study and report on racism in America.[67] When is the United Nations going to study and report on racism in South Africa and Zimbabwe? In the latter country, ruthless and corrupt leadership has murdered and driven away fifth-generation whites, stolen their land, and oppressed, starved, and killed much of the black populace, with no serious objection from and no action by the United Nations. Where was the United Nations during the murders of millions in Cambodia, Laos, and Vietnam in the 1970s? The UN is not the sort of organization to which any country,

67 Ahni, "UN Rapporteur Documenting Racism in the US," May 22, 2008, accessed August 11, 2011, *http://intercontinentalcry.org/un-rapporteur-documenting-racism-in-us/*.

especially the most powerful country in the world, should entrust its affairs. Congressional rhetoric about restoring America's alliances and restoring America's credibility in the world is, at best, so much political garbage. At worst, it calls for the voluntary relinquishment of American power and entrusting American interests to an organization that is ineffective as well as often hostile to American interests (for example, proclaiming that the Iraq war was illegal), despite receiving disproportionately great financial support from the United States.

In international relationships, it's not about friendships and bonhomie between countries. You can't like someone you're jealous of; and to my mind, jealousy and envy are two of the main emotions people outside our borders feel about us. Add covetousness to that, and you'll understand why commentators like Michael Savage, the host of a widely heard talk radio show, *The Savage Nation*, talk about the importance of the sanctity of our borders.

The aversion of American politicians to military force began soon after the Germans and Japanese surrendered in World War II. Roosevelt, in my opinion, foolishly allowed the Soviet Union to take over the Eastern European countries that became known as the Soviet bloc. It can be argued that the rebuilding and rehabilitation of Japan, in contrast, worked well because Alger Hiss and his like had no role in the reconstruction of Japan, a process of which General MacArthur was in charge. Japan committed its own atrocities during the war, yet is now one of the world's great democracies. The same sort of thinking that allowed the Iron Curtain to be established led many federal politicians to decide they favored pulling out of Iraq. They no doubt saw abandoning and vilifying Bush as in their best political interests. Such thinking today makes the leftist position on Iran and its growing atomic weapons capabilities one of endless negotiations, with no deadlines and no threat of force.

If American politicians understand that America needs to remain the dominant military power in the world, they have shown no sign. Why so many of them shrink from even the credible threat of military force is complicated, but not a mystery. There are powerful lobbies with unlimited money that advocate pacifism and appeasement, and they have purchased the allegiance of Democratic congresspeople. George Soros is only one of many rich and powerful forces on the Left who advocates a world with America as a greatly diminished power. In addition, as earlier noted, many federal legislators believe that the American people, as a whole, dislike war and would prefer for the country not to be involved in one. They also believe, with some validity, that a lot of Americans would like to see the defense budget cut, so that more money would be available for social programs. Regardless of the exact motivations, it is a fact that most Democratic senators and representatives, with support from Bush-jettisoning Republicans, advocated an end to the war in Iraq, regardless of the consequences to the Iraqi people, the region, and to our armed forces still in Iraq. They were willing to let Iraq descend into a bloody fiasco, and perhaps are willing to let Iran possess nuclear weapons, if they can thereby keep themselves in power.

We are facing serious threats to our safety, and even to our existence. Four squads of Middle Eastern Islamic fanatics, all but one of them Saudi Arabians, murdered nearly three thousand innocents and destroyed billions of dollars worth of our property in 2001. Iran, Hamas, Hezbollah, and others are itching to do it again, preferably on a bigger scale with real weapons. How blind can we be, how docile can we be, to let the Left and the current administration unilaterally diminish the strength and readiness of our military forces, while the House and Senate stand idly by?

We as Americans must understand that consistent, overwhelming military power and the willingness to use it are essential to our continued status as a dominant world power, and our ability to protect ourselves against potential aggression and possible annihilation. Herman Wouk, in *War and Remembrance*, volume 2, published in 1978 by Little, Brown and Company, stated through his main character, Admiral Victor Henry, what I believe to be the correct view of war: "The world now loathes the very thought of industrialized war, after two big doses of it," wrote Victor Henry in his fictional post-World War II memoir.

"Yet, while belligerent fools or villains anywhere on earth consider it an optional policy, what can free men do but confront them with what met the Japanese at Leyte Gulf, and Adolf Hitler in the skies over England in 1940—daunting force, and self-sacrificing brave spirits ready to wield it?"[68] If the United States of America continues to equivocate on this subject, continues to afford the Left and its elected lapdogs a choice in the matter, and continues to allow politicians like Senator Harry Reid to proclaim that we have lost a war while it was being fought, a war that we actually won, we are at grave risk. If we elect self-interested politicians who think diplomacy and negotiating with our enemies are a substitute for the credible and unequivocal threat of military force, we are doomed. Maybe not immediately, but doomed. Russia is a resurgent power, and I believe it is still furious about the humiliation it experienced when Reagan helped to bring about the downfall of the Soviet Union. Russia has enough oil, enough nuclear technology, and enough ruthlessness to regain the position it held during the 1960s. China has all of the makings of a dominant world power. It is possibly only a matter of time before China decides to conquer Taiwan, and dares us to do something about it. If that happens, our politicians will talk, but not act. That will be a national humiliation for us. And it might be only a short time before Iran has nuclear weapons, which it could sell or give to our enemies, including Islamic jihadists.

While this book is not intended as advocacy for any political position or party, it seems clear that at this time in world history, America's best interests lie in not electing candidates who are obligated to monied groups with extreme anti-military views, but in electing senators and representatives who will be free to vote in our best national interests, which many believe include being backed by a permanently powerful military. Having a strong military does not mean it has to be used indiscriminately. And, as discussed in chapter 5, a country cannot have a powerful military without a powerful economy. In my view, the only way to have a powerful economy is to encourage the most

68 Wouk, *War and Remembrance*, 2:1055.

successful, productive, and competent members of the private sector to do what they do best, without constricting regulation and onerous taxation. A college economics professor wrote recently that the decline of the once great nations was caused in part by "'bread and circuses,' where government spends money for the shallow and immediate wants of the population, and civic virtue all but disappears."[69] That would apply to, for example, legislation cutting military budgets so as to provide more free benefits to grateful voters. All such legislative decisions, however they turn out, need to be made by disinterested lawmakers whose minds and voting records are unencumbered by obligations and self-interest.

Our legislators are simply too concerned with their own futures to focus on and realistically evaluate the behavior of other nations. They are too attentive to and too obedient to wealthy and persuasive forces that do not believe the United States should have the means of avoiding war in a dangerous world by being too powerful to challenge. They are too willing to support military action at the outset and then undermine it later, all in reaction to polls and pressure from wealthy appeasers and pacifists. The only way we will ever have federal legislators who will use their own consciences, knowledge, intelligence, and belief systems in their voting choices will be to do away with any incentives to favor any single-issue group or to garner votes from voters who don't like war. The only way to do that is to deprive them of reelection.

---

69 Walter Williams, "Is U.S. on Verge of Joining the 'Once-Mighty,'" *Investor's Business Daily*, June 2, 2011.

CHAPTER 7

The Iraq War, Pandering Politicians, and Our Safety

The actual war in Iraq has been over since 2003. America won. The objective was to depose the regime of Saddam Hussein and replace it with a Democratically-elected government which would not be a threat to the Middle East and the rest of the free world. That objective has been accomplished. Iraq, in 2003 a brutal dictatorship and kleptocracy, is now the "only functioning Arab democracy."[70]

Despite some arguable success, there is a legitimate issue as to whether the war was a good or bad idea. This chapter offers no opinion on that. My concern is the politically motivated conduct of American legislative leaders that placed our fighting men and women in increased peril.

The Iraq war was undertaken with the official support of every major politician then serving in the United States Senate. What happened after that was not a war. It was a fragmented struggle on the part of selfish, sadistic, and extremist elements that were committed to preventing a parliamentary democracy from governing Iraq. The media euphemistically called the violent extremists an insurgency. It was more correctly called a violent criminal movement supported

70 Charles Krauthammer, "Bush Doctrine Stirs Middle East Revolts," *Orlando Sentinel*, March 6, 2011.

by a combination of frustrated Saddam loyalists, al-Qaeda members, Sunni radicals, Iran, Syria, and miscellaneous criminals of opportunity. The so-called insurgency and the determination of many Democrats and some Republicans to not allow our armed forces to crush it were among the reasons Republicans lost their majorities in the Senate and House of Representatives in 2006, and fared worse in the election in November 2008.

Even Bush had to admit that we had invaded a sovereign country that had not posed an immediate military threat to the United States. That fact has been the basis for a massive politicization of the entire matter. The Iraq War became a political tool for politicians to use to discredit the Bush administration and its aggressive approach to promoting freedom outside our borders. The prevailing view became that it had been an unnecessary war that had caused more harm than good. But let's remember that the 2003 Iraq War came about as an eventual result of Iraq's invasion of Kuwait more than a decade earlier. That unprovoked and vicious attack was the most blatant invasion of one sovereign country into another since Hitler's multiple invasions in World War II. Saudi Arabia, an authoritarian regime that is good at cutting off its own citizens' heads but has a lousy army, would have been next. Iraq, under Saddam Hussein, would have controlled oil supplies in the Middle East. *The unprovoked invasion of Kuwait was conclusive evidence that Hussein was an international criminal willing to use his country's armed forces to conquer a defenseless and wealthy neighbor and steal its wealth.* No serious person has ever argued that our national security was not jeopardized by that invasion.

In the years following the invasion of Kuwait, the United Nations, no fan of aggressive action against dictatorships, resolved seventeen times that Saddam would have to disarm and submit to inspections to verify disarmament. Over and over the United Nations issued resolutions to that effect, and again and again Saddam lied, dissembled, and at times simply refused. In the year or two before we invaded Iraq, all the leading Democrats, including Bill Clinton, Hillary Clinton, Tom Daschle, Al Gore, and John Kerry, stated that they believed Saddam had and would use biological weapons, chemical weapons, and/or nuclear weapons, otherwise known as weapons of mass destruction. Senators who voted to attack Iraq in 2002 had access to the same intelligence as Bush and his advisors. The foreign intelligence services of France, Germany, England, and others also maintained that Iraq was pursuing a program of nuclear and biological weapons. The claim that Bush lied about Iraq having the weapons at the time of the attack is false and malicious. A lie occurs when someone knows the facts and intentionally misstates them. There has never been a shred of evidence that Bush knew anything different from what the Clintons, Gore, Daschle, Kerry, France, England, and Germany said they knew. The claim that Bush lied on this subject is every bit as false as the claim put forward by a few lunatic fringe liberals, such as Cynthia McKinney, former representative of Georgia, that Bush knew about the September 11, 2001, attack beforehand and chose to let it happen. One problem, however, with the American people, is that if a malicious lie is spread for a long enough time, people will believe it and vote on the basis of it. That is one tactic some elected federal legislators use to stay in office, and one of many reasons for a one-term limit.

There is unrefuted evidence of at least three things about the weapons that have been so much in question. First, Saddam used chemical weapons to kill his own citizens, civilians who had harmed no one. No one disputes that. Second, evidence shows that he had and was stockpiling biological weapons; that is, weapons for spreading lethal diseases. Third, he had a nuclear reactor as early as 1980, which, happily, was destroyed by the Israelis. A great deal of other evidence indicates Saddam was trying to reassemble Iraq's nuclear capability. Does anyone seriously think, with Israel already in possession of such weapons and Iran making largely unimpeded efforts to do the same, that Saddam wasn't pursuing nuclear weaponry as hard as he could?

We won a quick military victory. We then ran into serious difficulties, because a large number of fanatics did not want Iraq to be a stable nation with stable politics and a sound economy; because Iran and Syria armed, equipped, and gave sanctuaries to these fanatics;

because the American Left successfully urged elected federal politicians to publicly and loudly oppose our war effort while our forces were in dangerous combat; and because we made mistakes we could have avoided.

According to Alan B. Krueger of Princeton University in a paper written in 2006, most of the armed militants were of domestic origin, although foreign fighters, such as Saudis, Kuwaiti, and Sudanese, played important roles in the violence. Sunni Arabs from within Iraq constituted most of the so-called insurgents.[71] Foreign fighters joined the local fanatics in bombings, ambushes and beheadings that were designed to thwart our and our allies' goal of a democratic and West-leaning Iraq. Those Islamist extremists did not want a representative government in Iraq that would have open and reasonable dealings with the rest of the planet. It is hard to know exactly what motivates the insurgents in Iraq, since such people do not freely or openly disclose their motives. It is safe to say that they want a fundamentalist, Taliban-type theocracy, such as the Taliban had in Afghanistan and the mullahs and ayatollahs have in Iran. Why they want that is not a mystery: they are driven by the same pathology that drove nineteen Arabs to murder 3,000 people in 2001. Those nineteen Arabs could not have begun or completed their mission without massive financial support from other Arabs, especially in Saudi Arabia, our alleged friend. It was not, then, happenstance that legions of Islamic jihadists, including al-Qaeda of Iraq, poured into Iraq, into a vacuum caused by the fall of the dictator who had held sway over the nation and its ravaged people. Given the motives behind 9/11 and earlier attacks on the World Trade Center and other targets, how could these extremists not have seized in 2003 the golden opportunity of a lifetime? The unthinkable thing, and a central point of this chapter, is that they almost succeeded. They may yet succeed, thanks to the political system of the country they so hate, the United States of America.

Despite the losses we suffered in Iraq, good things resulted. First,

71 Michael Eisenstadt and Jeffrey White, "Assessing Iraq's Sunni Insurgency," *Military Review* (May-June 2006).

an international terrorist nation, Libya, quickly moved over to our side. Our politicians don't want that talked about, and their allies in the mainstream media have refrained from doing so. But remember how from the late 1970s through the 1990s, Libya engaged in repeated acts of terrorism, including blowing up an airliner over Scotland, which killed more than two hundred people? During that time, Libya was the world's leading terrorist state. The timing of its turnaround strongly indicates that Bush's toughness, first toward Afghanistan and then Iraq, caused the Libyan strongman, Gadhafi, to see the light and decide that behaving, including abandoning a nuclear weapons program, was better than regime change in Libya.[72] Another result was that Syria removed its armed forces from Lebanon, a country it had occupied and dominated for decades. Lebanon then had elections. Free and fair elections were also held in Iraq and Afghanistan, while Egypt and Saudi Arabia at least recognized democratic movements. North Korea also suddenly decided to talk about dismantling its nuclear program, (a process that derailed in 2009).

Other good results are reported. As reported in an *Investor's Business Daily* article on March 20, 2008, and also in the CIA's *The World Factbook* from 2008, the economy of Iraq began growing after decades of stagnation. From 2002 through 2006, per capita gross domestic product rose 110 percent. Before the war, about 833,000 Iraqi households had telephones. By early 2008, about ten million people had them; and by 2010, about twenty-one million had a land line or a cell phone. Before the war, fewer than 5,000 people had Internet access. Today, hundreds of thousands of individuals enjoy that practice. Under Saddam's regime, there were no private television stations. Now there are more than fifty. Similarly, there are about 260 independent newspapers and magazines, while there were none under Saddam. For the first time since the Saddam Hussein regime, Iraq is undertaking legitimate business with the private oil industries of the world. In early 2010, successful national elections took place, involving thousands

72 "A Free Iraq Prevented Nuclear Libya," *Investor's Business Daily*, March 3, 2011.

of legitimate candidates and millions of voters who braved gunfire and bombs to go to the polls. As this is written, Iraq is in a political and electoral situation not unlike our own for several years after our war for independence. As in the case of our post-revolution founding, and unlike most changes of forms of government in the Middle East, none of the contending parties are threatening violence or a military takeover. In fact, "The Iraqis have surprised even themselves with their passion for democratic processes."[73]

While there is still violence, it is criminal violence, and it is being combated by a legitimate government. During Saddam's regime, an average of 50,000 Iraqis died each year at the hands of the government. Thanks to the West, a genocidal and kleptomaniacal government was replaced by an elected government that has laws and punishes criminals.

A legitimate question is what good has come so far of the Iraq War, and what good will follow.

If, as was planned by Bush, the Iraqi moderates consolidate power, maintain a stable government composed of Shiites, Sunnis, Kurds and fringe groups, and build a sound economy, the benefit will be enormous and enjoyed worldwide. Such a result will cause the monarchies and dictatorships in the Middle East, the world's most strategically important area and its primary trouble spot, to understand that they need to dial down the repression of their people, especially women; and that they need to move toward more open forms of government. Perhaps not legislative democracies, with the type of civil liberties we have, but nonetheless governments that provide some civil liberties and opportunities for the poor and oppressed to become middle class. Even the Democrats can't argue that that would not be a good result. Yet they claimed until 2009, even in the face of increasing evidence to the contrary, that it was not possible. Now they are seeking to claim credit for what increasingly is a good outcome.

Another immediate result was that our invasion and the aftermath

73 Babak Dehghanpisheh, "Rebirth of a Nation," *Newsweek*, February 26, 2010.

drew out into the open Islamic jihadists and terrorists of all varieties, and brought them into Iraq where they were fought against and killed. We no longer had to guess whether Iran and Syria are America's enemies. The thousands of explosive devices Iran sent to the extremists in Iraq may not have been weapons of mass destruction, but they destroyed a lot of American lives. One of the poorest leftist arguments was that by invading Iraq and by otherwise taking an aggressive stance toward terrorism, we made enemies we would not otherwise have. The attacks on September 11, 2001, were utterly unprovoked. The same is true of all other Islamic terrorist attacks that preceded 9/11, including the 1993 attack on the World Trade Center, the bombing of the USS Cole in Yemen, and all the other vicious attacks that killed so many innocent people and destroyed billions of dollars in property. The things we have difficulty accepting, because they are so horrible, is that *all* of those attackers were radical fundamentalist Muslims, that they have access to—and are seeking more access to—money and high-tech weaponry, and that they will succeed unless they are crushed and killed, every last one of them. They don't understand persuasion, they don't negotiate, they don't compromise, they don't wear uniforms and identify themselves, and they are now cruelly and viciously murdering small numbers of people in Iraq and around the world by stealth, because that's all they can accomplish for the moment. They are as ruthless as the barbarians that destroyed the Roman Empire, and the Vikings who sacked Europe and slaughtered its inhabitants. They are more difficult to deter, since the Visigoths and Vikings were only seeking loot. They did not have an ideological urge to change the world through death and destruction. The ambitious goal of the modern terrorists is too horrible to easily comprehend. It is the destruction of Western, especially American, civilization. It includes killing as many of us as possible, and destroying as much of our property as possible. "There are no concessions we can make that will buy off hate-filled terrorists ...They want our soul—and if they are willing to die, and we are not, they will get it."[74]

In light of the resources we have compared to what they have, that seems a difficult proposition. Anyone who thinks it can't happen, however, needs to study Gibbon's *Decline and Fall of the Roman Empire.* As earlier noted, Gibbon wrote that Rome was weakened not only by decadence, but by several centuries of military and political leaders killing their rivals for short-term personal gain. Our politicos are not doing that, but in many cases the vocal animosity of the so-called elected elites toward dissenters makes one see the parallel! Around the time of Christ, it would have seemed preposterous that northern and western European barbarians could have conquered and sacked Rome, but it happened only a few centuries later. With today's weaponry and technology, things happen a lot faster.

But, the American Left will say, unlike Ancient Rome, we are not threatened by contiguous and hostile nations or peoples. So what? Our borders are sieves. The Left is pushing for immigration reform that would legalize millions of impoverished illegal immigrants. It is a self-deluding fantasy to think our uninvited immigrants do not include enemies with dangerous contraband. A well-placed nuclear bomb that took out centers of communications and government power; a fast-spreading, epidemic-causing germ; a poisonous gas effectively disseminated; and fifty or sixty thousand well-armed fanatics who crossed over from Mexico and Canada, hidden in our population centers with automatic weapons ... You get the picture. It is a scientific fact that one nuclear warhead detonated over the United States could send out an electromagnetic pulse that would destroy our technological infrastructure and send us and our economy back to the eighteenth century, causing mass death and unimaginable destruction.[75] With this grim fact in mind, what happened on September 11, 2001, should be

74 Thomas Sowell, "Roman Empire Outlasted U.S., But It Too Fell," *Investor's Business Daily*, December 10, 2008.

75 "The Next 9/11 – A Nuclear One?," *Investor's Business Daily*, September 12, 2011.

seen as a warning. We need to get serious. We do not need appeasement-minded and semi-loyal politicians elected by MoveOn.org. We need conscientious legislators who want to protect our country.

The Iraq issue cannot be assessed by taking a snapshot of the difficulties we had with the murderous fanatics who gathered there. We had the means for squashing them, but politicians beholden to the Left got in our way. The American people need to wake up and realize that we already had enemies; we could not avoid having them; and that attacking them when they cross borders to attack us, as they did in Iraq, and destroying their resources does not create more enemies. That sequence of events simply places enemies in positions where they can be killed. If that is done effectively, it will frustrate them and deny them their heinous goals. It shows them and the entire world that America won't stand still and be destroyed. Instead, America will defend itself. And if the American Left will stand back and let the armed forces and conscientious federal legislators do their jobs, we will destroy enough of them, as well as their sources of money and weapons, so as to be a lot safer than we are now.

Regardless of whether the Iraq War ultimately turns out to have been a good thing, I contend that the almost traitorous commentary on the subject by politicians obligated to the American Left damaged the war effort and cost American and Iraqi lives. No reasonable person can argue that when national figures, such as United States senators, are critical of the American war effort, it encourages the enemy. When a Secretary of Defense is called before a Senate committee during wartime, and posturing ideologues are allowed to ask him whether it's time he be fired, it's hard to make your enemies think they should stop murdering American soldiers and innocent Iraqi civilians. I cannot believe that the main purpose behind that was not political. It would not have happened if those senators had been serving their only term in office.

Of course, it is also harmful when a grief-stricken pawn like Cindy Sheehan and a pacifist organization like MoveOn.org receive worldwide coverage for calling Bush the worst terrorist of all, and accusing him of genocide. Harry Reid, Senator Barack Obama, Nancy Pelosi, the *New York Times*, some Hollywood celebrities, and the leftist 527 groups kept on criticizing the war, because they knew that any American lives lost due to their conduct could not be proven to be their fault. That does not mean their conduct was anything other than reprehensible. At this time, whether one was for or against the war, it is a known fact that we deposed the Saddam Hussein regime; that we and the newly free Iraqis are nearly finished stamping out the cowardly, murderous thugs who were murdering and maiming our soldiers and their own countrymen; and that it looks like the Iraqis are not going to suffer another military takeover or let the remaining fanatics deprive them of their country. We have done this despite the contrary advocacy of federal legislators, including some Republicans (Chuck Hagel, John Warner, and others), who appeared to be invested in our defeat and withdrawal. Such politicians are entitled to their opinions, but their actions should not be poll-driven or Soros-funded, with a further term in office as their goal.

There are several things we might have done to procure a less costly and time-consuming positive outcome in Iraq.

First, while the surge was an unqualified success, and doubtless a disappointment to some on the Left, the discussion of timetables for troop reductions was a mistake. That simply encouraged the enemy. If you were playing a football game against a superior team and losing, but you knew that in the second half its starters would all be benched and scrubs would play the rest of the game, that would encourage you to play harder.

We needed to take measures so that our soldiers would not be afraid of being court-martialed or tried in civilian courts for any aggressive tactics they used in defeating our enemies. (And, as this is written, our combat troops in Afghanistan need to ask lawyers if it is okay to shoot armed enemies.) There is something seriously wrong when hardships endured by vicious killers in prison in Iraq and Guantanamo Bay get more media coverage and more attention from United States authorities than beheadings of innocent Americans by terrorists in Iraq.

Because some of the insurgents arrived from Syria or Iran, we also needed to secure the borders between those countries and Iraq and do whatever it takes, including the use of air power, to maintain the security of those borders. According to a December 19, 2006, report prepared for Congress by Kenneth Katzman of Congressional Research Service, the explosives, explosives experts, weapons, and money were not produced only in Iraq; they came from Iran. Iran knowingly helped carry on the insurgency, and was directly responsible for the killing of our men and women in uniform.

The Bush administration might have done those things, except for the opposition of the Left and its for-hire lawmakers. When the Senate voted for the war, that was an indication to the world that we had stopped worrying about what France and the United Nations thought about our foreign policy. We needed to resume that attitude and take whatever measures are necessary with Syria and Iran, including acts of war, to end the flow into Iraq of foreign killers, explosives, weapons, and financing. Without the insurgency, Iraq, with its inherent wealth, would be well on its way to prosperity and some form of democratic government.

We failed to do these things because politics got in the way. The war, like all wars, became unpopular, and President Bush was turned into a figure of hate. It became politically advantageous for the elected officials who helped start the war to criticize it, and to interfere with its fully effective prosecution. Discrediting Bush became more important than protecting our armed forces and sealing our victory.

We always had the capability of winning this war, as we did the Vietnam War. Both times, as I see it, politics interfered. We cannot, especially now, afford to lose this fight and fall into another three-decade hand-wringing, anti-military funk. We might not survive it. The facts that the going is tough and lives are still being lost are grim, and it is regrettable that a lot of that could have and should have been prevented. But now we need to quit debating whether we are going to successfully finish the job in Iraq, and just do it. We simply can't let the Left, with its America-is-bad agenda, dictate our future.

With respect to the Iraq War, whether it was a good thing or a bad thing is still a matter of intense debate. [76] If you hate Bush, the war is the same terrible mistake it was before it even began, and you keep attacking it. If you were a Bush lemming, it continues to be a holy crusade and you don't question it. But let's look at reality. Saddam Hussein defied the UN more than a dozen times, and if we did nothing else in ousting him, we proved that for once a series of UN resolutions would be enforced. Everyone from Bill Clinton to John Kerry to the UN believed and stated he was making and stockpiling WMD. We rid the world and the Iraqi people of one of the most ruthless, sadistic, and brutal dictators the world has ever experienced. The only people in Iraq who are still unhappy about his downfall are those people who benefited from his rule.

We also saw, right after the invasion and even today, dynamic new economic growth all over the Middle East, with dramatically increasing foreign investment. That's the big key to loosening the grips of despotic Islamic rulers and letting citizens of those countries become free and prosperous. Wealth is power, wealth is freedom. Free, prosperous, and happy people don't support suicide attacks on crowds of innocent civilians or office towers. We will not see the end of Islamic jihad until the wealth of Middle Eastern nations is no longer concentrated in the hands of royal families, theocratic mullahs, heads of state, and their chosen cronies.

One of the persistent themes from the Bush-hating war critics is that the war was "really about oil," and that the United States wanted to control or own Iraq's oil reserves. There is, however, absolutely no evidence of that. We lost lives and billions of dollars rebuilding infrastructure so that Iraq can begin making money from its oil reserves. In the process, we have forgiven a lot of Iraqi debt, and we have incurred a lot of anger from European nations by pressuring them to do the

76 A September 7, 2004, op-ed in the *Orlando Sentinel* by a Princeton University assistant professor stated that "the Bush solution of reforming the Middle East to combat terrorism is the only serious plan on the table," and that Senator Kerry had no plan.

same. We and many other Western nations are and will continue to be dependent on foreign oil. As long as Iraq controls and benefits from its oil supply, why shouldn't the United States enjoy a major and lasting influence on Iraq, as well as other oil-producing nations, such as Saudi Arabia and its neighbors in the Arabian Peninsula? If we don't, it will be the Chinese, the Russians, or Iran. Two of those countries are rivals of ours who are not constrained by our rules, and Iran has been our declared enemy since 1979. Someone will end up with a long-lasting and mutually beneficial economic relationship with Iraq. Why should it not be us? Do George Soros, Al Franken, and various members of the Left hate America so much that they want it to have a lower standard of living?

If all goes well, in another ten years we will know that the Iraq War had the following effects: (1) the deaths of tens of thousands of our sworn enemies; (2) stabilization of the entire Middle East; (3) allowing the people of the Middle East to be able to live in freedom and following their own aspirations, instead of the wishes of brutal dictators; (4) bringing about a new economic health and prosperity to the region; (5) helping to do away with the dangerous, fanatical Islamic extremism that threatens lives and property in all parts of the world; and (6) creating and maintaining for the United States and its allies opportunities to transact oil and other business with Iraq and its neighbors. Also, it will have helped save our one true ally in the region, Israel. If we had turned tail and run in Iraq as we did in Vietnam, we would have kissed Israel good-bye.

None of this—other than item (1)—will happen as long as senators and representatives act on the wishes of the American Left and voters who view wars as bad and think that our defense budget should be slashed. The story of our involvement in Iraq has significance beyond what happens in and to Iraq. It has significance beyond what happens in the Middle East, although that, as discussed in the next chapter on Iran, is of critical importance. The sad fact is that some of our politicians allowed our success in Iraq to be less important than discrediting the administration of George W. Bush and Dick Cheney. Only those who are committed to leftist politics believe that the incessant and vicious criticism of the war did not increase the physical risks to our armed forces. Those who did the criticizing from positions of high elected office are safe, because the harmful effects of their activities cannot be proven. Nonetheless, between 2003 and 2008, I feel that the politicians dominated by the American Left showed that their short-term political interest, driven by the ideology of their supporters, was more important to them than the safety of our armed forces and the long-term safety and welfare of the American public.

America was protected between 2003 and the end of the Bush administration from terrorist attacks, in spite of interference from the American Left and its paid-for federal politicians. There is legitimate reason for the American public to consider whether it can trust politicians at the federal level who are so obligated to far-left causes. Between our lax and loosely enforced immigration laws, the proliferation of nuclear arms, and the vast amounts of monies available worldwide to America-hating terrorists, there is far more reason to fear a devastating attack than anyone in either chamber of Congress has discussed. Our country will be in clear danger unless and until our federal legislators cease seeking careers in office, and until they vote with independent judgment, with no obligation to anyone, and in sole reliance on known facts and their America-bred consciences. The issues discussed in this chapter relating to the Iraq experience and terrorist acts of war should have been decided by senators and representatives who were unconcerned with reelection. That is prominent among the reasons they must have only the one term.

CHAPTER 8

Iran: Looming Disaster

When the United States invaded Iraq in 2003, Iran was not on our radar screen. It should have been. Iran has been our enemy since 1979, when armed militants, almost certainly acting at the express direction of the new ruler, Ayatollah Ruholla Khomeini, stormed and occupied the United States embassy in Tehran. The militants held the embassy staff hostage for over one year. According to Ali Khameini, the Supreme Leader of Iran, his country has been in a "state of war" with the United States since 1979.[77] Our current administration has belatedly acknowledged that Iran is and has been assisting al-Qaeda in its deadly designs against the United States.[78] The 1979 takeover of our embassy and Iran's becoming an Islamic dictatorship that treats its own people "with total contempt"[79] were made possible by a mistake our government has made before—backing a new revolutionary leader over an established ally. In the case of Iran, its shah had been a dictator, but he was allied with our country. The situation in the Middle East would be entirely different today, and much more to our liking, had President Jimmy Carter not favored Ayatollah Khomeini and made it possible for

77 Michael Ledeen, "Understanding Iran," *Imprimis*, October 2008, Vol. 37, Number 10.

78 "Al Qaeda in Iran," *Wall Street Journal*, July 29, 2011.

79 Ledeen, "Understanding Iran."

him and his fanatical followers to overcome the shah and establish a theocratic dictatorship that has declared its hatred of the United States and its intent to annihilate our ally, Israel. President Eisenhower made the same mistake years earlier, when the United States tolerated the ascent of Fidel Castro over the Cuban strongman Fulgencio Batista, on the grounds that Batista was a dictator. He was a dictator, but he and Cuba were also our allies. Castro, after taking power, revealed that he was a committed communist, and he had thousands of his countrymen executed.[80] He allied Cuba with the Soviet Union for many years, until Soviet Union's economic collapse made supporting Cuba an unaffordable luxury.

Carter, for the remainder of his presidency, allowed Iran to humiliate our country. Proving a point made in chapter 6 of this book, Iran promptly released the hostages when Ronald Reagan became president. Khomeini knew that the fun was over, and that effective military action would soon result from continuing to hold the hostages.

Since then, Iran has sponsored and funded terrorist groups that are enemies of liberal democracies in general and Israel in particular. These groups include Hamas and Hezbollah. Anyone who does not understand that Iran has furnished billions of dollars and untold amounts of weapons to those groups is either ignorant or heavily invested in leftist politics. Throughout the Iraq War, Iran directly and indirectly furnished explosives that killed and maimed hundreds, if not thousands, of our fighting men and women.[81] We have done nothing in response to these acts of war.[82]

For nearly a decade it has been clear that Iran is in the process of developing nuclear weapons. Iran is lying when it claims that its nuclear program is exclusively for the purpose of producing power for internal use. There is no reason for Iran not to lie, and many reasons for

---

80 "Minor Atrocities of the Twentieth Century," last updated July 2005, accessed August 1, 2011, http://users.erols.com/mwhite28/warstat6.htm.

81 David S. Cloud, "Weapons from Iran Have 'really hurt us,'" *Orlando Sentinel*, July 11, 2011.

82 "Rip Van Clinton," *Investor's Business Daily*, March 4, 2011.

it to lie. After all, the United States did not publicize the Manhattan Project. The first public knowledge of that came when we exploded a nuclear device over Japan at the end of World War II. As I point out in chapter 6, not only do sovereign nations act in their own interests when they have the power to do so, they also conceal or lie about their true intentions. If they do not, they fail to achieve their national objectives.

As I write this, the United States and Western Europe continue to dither and blather about sanctions against Iran—sanctions that are hurting the people of Iran, but which are not interfering with the goals, or even the comfort, of the ruling elites. Russia and China continue to obstruct our efforts to impose further sanctions. Russia and China have also recently become formally allied with Iran, and vice versa, in opposing US missile defense initiatives.[83] Estimates vary as to when Iran will have nuclear weapons and the capability to deliver them. Some say one year, some say ten years, but it really does not matter. When that happens, as it will unless we and Israel take military action, Iran will rule the Middle East. Even if it does not attack Israel, it will threaten to annihilate any country in the region that does not do its bidding. That will include Saudi Arabia and the other oil-producing countries, which would be largely powerless to resist. It is foreseeable that Iran, armed with nuclear weapons, will control the oil supply from the Middle East. The United States could be cut off. As a result, oil could cost us $200-$300 per barrel. Another likely result would be that our military would be largely crippled, since oil could be in short supply and there are no alternative energy sources for our military machines. Read that again: there are no fuels for our tanks, humvees, jet fighters, jet bombers, and transport aircraft other than those produced from oil. Similarly, the standard of living in our country would diminish dramatically. Anyone living in this country who does not believe that will happen if Iran obtains nuclear weapons is either hopelessly ignorant, in favor of that happening, or blinded by far-left ideologies.

---

83 "Ahmadinejad's New Friends," *Investor's Business Daily*, June 16, 2011.

A related and even more serious problem is the prospect that Iran, with nuclear weaponry in hand, will sell or give such weapons to groups wishing to harm the United States. In the April 4, 2011, edition of *Investor's Business Daily*, an article entitled "The Real Radiation Hazard: Iran" contained the observation that "the most likely source for an eventual nuclear terrorist attack on the U.S. or Europe is Iran." It also stated that the many "rounds of economic sanctions have been laughably ineffective." In fact, a former adviser to Democratic presidents and the founding dean of the John F. Kennedy School of Government at Harvard, Graham Allison, was quoted in the article as warning that "detonation of a terrorist nuclear device in an American city is inevitable if the U.S. continues on its present course."[84] Indeed, in that Iran is willing to furnish, as it has, explosives to kill and maim our troops in Iraq, it does not take a genius to foresee Iran furnishing nuclear weapons to America-hating terrorists programmed to do Iran's dirty work without Iran seeming accountable. One scenario is Iran furnishing a nuclear warhead, a missile, and technical assistance to a terrorist group, and the armed missile being launched from a civilian vessel in international waters to be detonated over the United States. As mentioned in chapter 7, such a detonation at the right altitude could produce an electromagnetic pulse that would radiate to the surface, destroy electronic circuits, and "wreak devastation on [our] technological, electrical and transportation infrastructure."[85] US Senator Jon Kyl calls that "the one way we could lose the war on terror."[86] Such massive destruction, inflicted by stealth, would in my opinion place our very sovereignty at risk.

A legitimate question is, why, in light of this and other threats, do we allow the categorically anti-war, anti-military Left to have partial control of our legislative process? To the Left and its minions in Congress, it seems to make no difference that Iranian President

84 "The Real Radiation Hazard: Iran," *Investor's Business Daily*, April 4, 2011.

85 "Iran Plans for a World without America," *Investor's Business Daily*, August 5, 2011.

86 Ibid.

Ahmadinejad is on record as envisioning "a world without America," and as having disclosed that Iran has a "war preparation plan" for "the destruction of Anglo-Saxon civilization."[87]

Pundits as well as government officials have claimed that military action against Iran would be ineffective. To my mind, that means such action would work just fine, but that for some reason it should not be done. Although force is the only thing that would cause Iran to alter its behavior, our government is relying on talk and sanctions that accomplish nothing. Secretary of State Clinton has already publicly said that Iran will join the A-Bomb Club, and that further diplomacy, sanctions, and "containment" are the only available remedies. To the extent that the American Left can influence a compliant, self-perpetuating Congress, Iran will continue on its way to becoming a nuclear power, taking control of the Middle East, and doing grave damage to our way of life. Iran poses a serious threat to the United States, and that is another reason why we need federal lawmakers who are beholden to nothing other than their own consciences and their ability to think.

---

87 Ibid.

CHAPTER 9

The Labor Unions

The largest group of supporters of liberal and left-wing congressional candidates is labor unions.[88] Unlike trial lawyers, who at least contribute money they have earned with their own efforts to politicians of their choosing, union officials hand over their members' money to elect senators and representatives that the unions choose to support. Also unlike trial lawyers, who by and large operate within the law, labor unions have a long history of theft, bribery, coercion, violence, and overall corruption, unheard of in any other type of American organization. The International Brotherhood of Teamsters, for example, has been under federal supervision for years, having admitted in a consent decree that it was under the control of organized crime. Despite their often sordid history, labor unions are a major force in American government because of the money they give to support candidates for Congress. It would benefit Americans to know a little about these organizations.

Labor unions have been around for a long time. They and their supporters in Congress try to sell the story that labor unions exist for the benefit of American workers, and to protect workers from greedy and abusive employers. Nothing could be further from the truth. Labor

88 Mark Hemingway, "Unions Are the Big Dogs of Campaign Spending," *San Francisco Examiner*, October 24, 2010.

unions, like all other money-making organizations, exist for their own benefit. They are for-profit organizations trying to sell their services for money.

The essential difference between labor unions and ordinary business organizations is the value created, or not created. Labor unions exist to persuade or force employers to pay more money to employees for their contributions to the business effort than the market for labor would otherwise require. Unions also seek to require employers to apply work rules that make the work easier and diminish productivity. Such activities create nothing of value. Business entities, on the other hand, make products or provide services that they sell, in accordance with the law of supply and demand, to customers and clients for money. Those activities in and of themselves create and add value, and enough of them add shareholder value.

Labor unions come in two varieties, private sector and public sector. Private-sector unions, also called industrial unions, deal with private employers, large and small, under federal legislation called the National Labor Relations Act (NLRA). Membership in private-sector unions has been declining for decades. Public-sector unions, on the other hand, are gaining members, money, and power. Public-sector unions are those that deal with states, counties, cities, towns, and other state and local government employers. Teachers' unions, which are thought by many to be partly responsible for the decline in American education, are public sector unions. There is a hybrid form of the public-sector union that, believe it or not, deals with agencies of the federal government such as the United States Postal Service. Even the employees of the National Labor Relations Board (NLRB) have their own union!

The only legitimate purpose of any labor union is to represent employees in collective bargaining with their employers over matters of wages, hours, and other conditions of employment. The NLRA was passed by Congress in 1935 to make it easier for unions to organize private-sector employees, and to give unions the legal right to demand collective bargaining with employers. Its stated purpose was to reduce "industrial strife" by facilitating the organization of employees by unions and the negotiation of collective bargaining agreements between unions and employers. By minimizing industrial strife, Congress meant minimizing strikes and work stoppages. Whether the act accomplished that purpose is debatable, in light of the enormous number of strikes that have occurred since its passage and which continue to occur every year, often with accompanying union-orchestrated violence.

The NLRA and similar laws passed by many states provide a procedure for unions to seek out employees of businesses or public entities, such as municipalities, and the steps for a secret ballot election among employees, held by the federal government or a state agency. If a majority of employees vote in favor of the union, the union is certified by the agency as the exclusive collective bargaining representative of the employees. That means that the employer has the legal duty to deal with the union about all conditions of employment, and is barred from dealing directly with any employee. Under federal and state law, neither party is required to agree to a proposal that it believes is against its interest, although unions don't necessarily mention that important fact when they organize employees.

In the private sector, if there is an impasse in bargaining, the employer is entitled to implement its final offer, and the union's only recourse is to call a strike. In a strike, the workers do not get paid by the employer. If the strike is purely over economic issues, as opposed to a violation of law committed by the employer, the employer can replace the strikers. That means the striking employees can lose their jobs. The union officials who called the strike continue to get paid.

In the 1960s, unions and various academics developed the notion that states should pass laws patterned on the NLRA, so that state and local government employees could have the benefit of collective bargaining, albeit at the expense of taxpayers. Many such laws were passed. The cost to the public has been astronomical, due to wages and benefits, out-of-control pension obligations, and the direct and indirect costs of dealing with an adversary in the workplace. As this is written, states and municipalities, faced with insolvency, are frantically trying to undo agreements their leaders negotiated with public employee unions, under which employees' wages and benefits, including unfunded retirement obligations, enormously exceed private-sector compensation for similar work.

In the public sector, the bargaining obligation is the same as in industry. Each side is required to bargain in good faith, but neither is required to agree to something it believes to be against its best interests. In the event of an impasse in bargaining, however, the procedure is different. Strikes and work stoppages are not allowed. With the federal government and in most states, striking by a public employee is a discharge offense. President Ronald Reagan dealt the labor movement a blow by firing the federally employed air traffic controllers for unlawfully striking in 1981. (The Left never forgave him.) In some states, unresolved collective bargaining issues are settled unilaterally by elected officials, such as a city or county commission. In other states and in federal agencies, such impasses are settled by interest arbitration, a process in which an arbitrator forces a compromise.

As stated earlier, the notion that private- and public-sector labor unions exist and operate for the benefit of employees is a myth. Good employees don't need unions. Good workers advance in an organization, private or public, on merit. Good employees are held back by union rules and by contract provisions insisted on by unions. Unions, to the extent they benefit employees at all, benefit mediocre and poor employees, who are typically protected from discharge by contracts that make it difficult and expensive to discharge employees. Unions are as invariably opposed to differences in pay based on job performance as they are to free-trade treaties.

The only realistic way to view unions is as business organizations that exist to advance their own interests. There are dozens of major labor unions, and hundreds of smaller ones. Some of the major ones are the Teamsters, the Laborers International Union, the Service Employees International Union (SEIU), and various construction trade unions. Every union has a president, vice presidents, and other officers. These individuals receive high salaries and excellent benefits, and in many cases they receive other payments that are hard to detect. The unions have large numbers of other employees who receive salaries and benefits. One of the few helpful labor laws passed by Congress is the Labor Management Reporting and Disclosure Act, which requires labor unions to file reporting forms with the Department of Labor every year. These forms detail information such as the salaries and other allowances paid to officers and employees. The reporting and disclosure requirements apply to international unions as well as local unions. Reviewing those reports can be shocking, and is not for the fainthearted. There are numerous instances of union officials being paid huge salaries, and then also receiving generous bonuses and allowances of one sort or another.

The important fact is that this money, unlike the money paid to corporate officers and management employees, does not come from making a product or providing a service. The dollars come instead from membership dues and, in some cases, fees paid by union members. Union dues are paid voluntarily only in states that have Right to Work laws. A Right to Work state is one in which, by law, an employee represented by a union is not required to join the union and pay dues. Unions hate this, and for many years have tried to persuade Congress to repeal Section 14(b) of the NLRA, which authorizes states to pass Right to Work laws. This, despite the fact that in the twenty-two Right to Work states, average GDP growth is higher and unemployment rates are lower than in "closed shop" states.[89] Many states that have industries with private-sector union representation are not Right to Work states. In those states, unions can force employees, within a short period of time after being hired, to join and pay dues. The dues typically amount to hundreds of dollars per year, no small sum for a worker paid by the hour. There are thousands of collective bargaining relationships between employers and unions in which the employees are forced to pay dues. In most such relationships, the employer is not paying any more money to the employees than it would if there were no union. To the unions, that is irrelevant. The employees still must pay dues.

89 Herman Cain, "How Unions Dis Taxpayers," *Investor's Business Daily*, May 3, 2011.

In all collective-bargaining relationships, industries spend enormous sums of money on human resources directors, labor negotiators, labor lawyers, labor consultants, and other individuals who assist and advise employers in labor negotiations. Staff employees also have to be paid to handle any grievances and arbitrations that arise. No one has ever calculated the cost of collective bargaining to American industry. It is an embedded cost, like taxes, but I am sure it is in the hundreds of billions of dollars per year, a not insignificant fraction of our annual gross domestic product. That money could be paid instead to the employees and shareholders. Employees have a hard time figuring that out, and unions of course don't want them to know. Some of that money also could go back into the companies for research and development of new products and processes, something desperately needed in our country. One of the many things that the union-supported members of Congress don't want us to think about is that millions of American families own shares, either directly or through their retirement plans, in thousands of companies that are spending unnecessary money, first on collective bargaining with unions and then on defending the many legal proceedings that result from such relationships.

The situation is even worse in the public sector. When the NLRA was passed, no one contemplated that a right to union representation would ever extend to state and local government employees, let alone federal employees. That has happened since the 1960s. It has been a gold mine for unions, for several reasons. First, union membership in the private sector has declined significantly, causing labor unions to lose revenue and influence. Among the reasons for that are increased automation in manufacturing. Another is that American executives have learned that it is to their advantage to treat employees well, so private-sector workers perceive less need for unions. Another reason is that private-sector industries tend to resist union organization, and have learned to do so effectively. A business organization, regardless of whether it is producing products or services, operates more efficiently without a third party wedged between the company and the employees, attempting to negotiate on behalf of the employees. Businesses, after all, are providing goods and services needed by the American public. If they produce goods and services that are not needed, they cease to exist. The operation of the free market tends to weed out for-profit businesses that are so inefficiently or unfairly operated that they attract labor unions, which are able to persuade the employees to elect them as bargaining agents.

Union membership in the public sector, on the other hand, has greatly expanded. In states such as Florida that have collective-bargaining laws, almost all public school teachers are unionized. Teachers' unions aggressively fight virtually all education reforms, including merit-based pay, testing students for achievement, and, of course, government-funded or privately funded vouchers for students who want to attend private schools rather than failing public schools. President Obama, with the support of the Democratically controlled Congress, cancelled the voucher program in the District of Columbia, which had benefited numerous poor students, many of them black. That was done at the request of teachers' unions. (So much for politicians' support of poor families when there are votes to be bought.) Increasing numbers of state and local government workers have been unionized by aggressive unions such as the SEIU and the American Federation of State, County and Municipal Employees. One reason why those unions and their memberships are expanding is that governments are not required to operate efficiently in order to remain in existence. Instead of having to earn profits to make ends meet, they have the power to tax. It's our tax money taken by force of law that is being spent on public-sector collective bargaining, not privately earned money that, when spent, reduces or cancels a margin of profit. A corollary to that is the inherent conflict of interest in public-sector unionism that does not exist in the private sector. Public employers are controlled by elected politicians who, like federal lawmakers, want to be reelected. In my experience, executives and managers hired by local and state governments want to operate efficiently, including in dealing with unions. But the local and state politicians know that public-sector unions have their members' money to spend on elections, and those politicians often are responsible for imprudent generosity—at public expense—to unionized employees in exchange for union electoral support. That is a major reason for the spread of public-sector unionism, as well as the financial plight of many states and cities.

Another reason for the growth of public-sector unionism is that public employers, including the federal government, state governments, and local governments, typically do not resist union organization. Their feeling seems to be that unions are inevitable. That is encouraged in part by the fact that the government hires numerous employees to handle the many grievances and other day-to-day issues that result from public-sector collective bargaining. Such employees, once hired and on the payroll, have no interest in seeing their roles diminished or eliminated, and in fact have considerable interest in expanding them. Therefore, labor unions are tolerated and even encouraged to a much greater extent in the public sector than in private industry.

This book is not meant to be about labor unions, any more than it is about environmentalists, trial lawyers, or other groups that support elected politicians. The point of this chapter is to expose the power that labor unions, both private sector and public sector, wield over elected legislators. It is to the great detriment of our country that these member-funded organizations have such control over members of Congress. Labor unions are not only against the free-trade agreement with Colombia; they are against all free trade. They claim that free-trade agreements deprive American workers of employment. What they really mean is that free-trade agreements actually increase opportunities in America for employment, but not necessarily in positions that lend themselves to union organization. Unions, you see, are interested only in gaining access to more individuals who can be persuaded or forced to pay membership dues. All labor unions are like all businesses, focused on making as much money as they can, and having as much control as possible over important decisions that affecting them. While their retirement funds, health and welfare funds, and apprenticeship funds are riddled with theft and corruption, their political action funds operate with machinelike precision. Enormous amounts of money are extracted from union members and directed to left-leaning politicians and causes. This happens, I believe, not because union officials have any real political philosophy, but because most Democrats, unlike most Republicans, are willing to pass legislation that unions want and kill legislation they don't want. Even President Obama has admitted his allegiance to labor unions![90]

As earlier noted, for decades unions have supported legislation that would allow them to force employees to join unions and pay money. An example of legislation that unions want is a proposal currently in Congress misleadingly called the Employee Free Choice Act (EFCA). The very name is a lie. Since passage of the NLRA, employees have voted by secret ballot in NLRB-conducted elections on whether they want union representation. Unions and employers campaign before an election, although the NLRB and federal courts regulate what employers can say. When employees who have signed union cards realize that the union cannot force their employer to agree to anything against its interests, and that union representation will cost them money, they often end up voting against union representation. The EFCA would allow union organizers to organize; and if a majority of employees are signed up, the employer would be forced by law to recognize the union, even without an election. The unions and their congressional supporters float the story that if employees are allowed to vote in a secret ballot election, employers and their attorneys will coerce them into voting against the union. This is despite the fact that coercion of employees by management in any matters related to labor unions is strictly forbidden and is penalized by law. It is also unnecessary. In my experience, a well-managed employer can win a NLRB election without unfair persuasion. The truth is that unions want employees to hear only their side of the story. They want to deprive employers of the opportunity to state the entire picture, and give employees the opportunity to understand the true nature of collective bargaining before voting, which is why they pushed so hard for the EFCA in 2009 and 2010.

90 Barack Obama, *The Audacity of Hope* (New York: Vintage Books, 2008), 141 ("I owe those Unions.").

A less known but equally costly and destructive part of the EFCA is a provision that would stifle collective bargaining based on the interests of both parties and their relative bargaining power. It provides that after 120 days of bargaining, all unresolved contract articles will be decided and imposed by a federal arbitrator. So much for freedom of contract.

The Employee Free Choice Act is one of the greatest frauds elected politicians have ever tried to perpetrate on American business and the American workforce. President Obama wholeheartedly supports this potential law; McCain would have vetoed it. The unions are desperately seeking its passage. If it passes, responsibility for that despicable act will lie with the members of Congress who voted for it on the orders of their masters in the labor unions.

At the risk of being redundant, labor unions should not be allowed to dictate important social and industrial policy. They should especially not be able to do that with their members' hard-earned money, particularly members in non-right-to-work states, who are forced to pay dues as a condition of their employment. This is one of the many compelling reasons why federal elected officials should no longer experience the distracting and corrupting luxury of reelection.

CHAPTER 10

The Environment, the Environmentalists, and the Politicians

The most fundamental and important considerations about the earth's environment are that the earth is largely covered by salt water; that much of its land mass is uninhabitable; that the usable and habitable land area is finite; that the earth's population and its demand for fresh water, food, energy, and living space are increasing; and that human colonization of outer space remains science fiction. In some parts of the world famine and starvation are already part of daily life. At some future time, the earth and its civilizations will face catastrophe because of these unchangeable factors.

In comparison to those factors, attempts to control, by legislation and regulation, changes in world climate—such as global warming, allegedly caused by industrial emissions—are a side issue. Although important, renewed exploration and drilling for oil, construction of new oil refineries, and increasing the use of nuclear energy to generate electricity are temporary fixes compared to what will probably happen in a final reckoning. Nonetheless, all of the strident advocacy and political noise-making by environmentalists is about neutralizing global warming, no oil exploration, no nuclear power, diversion of water supplies from production of food in order to save a species of minnow and other such issues. To my knowledge, no environmental group has ever suggested that the destruction of civilization could be delayed or avoided if people around the world who cannot support their children would cease having so many children. Such advocacy would be seen as racist and otherwise politically incorrect. That alone tells us that a lot of the environmentalists' advocacy is of a political rather than scientific nature.

Instead of talking about measures that would delay an unthinkable world catastrophe, the environmentalists have sought to close scientific debate on a highly debatable subject. Some of the main proponents of global warming and its alleged harmful effects on the environment are politicians, not scientists. Al Gore won worldwide acclaim for a documentary film about global warming that was so flawed, Great Britain did not allow it to be shown at schools without disclaimers explaining the errors. For that reason, its producers do not show it in Great Britain. While some qualified scientists suspect that the earth's temperature is being affected by industrial emissions, many others have stated that there is either no such thing as man-caused global warming, or that its effect is too small to be cause for concern. They base that analysis on empirical evidence. The proof that the subject has become political, instead of remaining solely scientific, is that the proponents of global warming and of climate-related regulation of American industry have done the very unscientific thing of seeking to close all further scientific inquiry and debate. Science consists of gathering data and evidence, discussing them, and performing scientific analyses to reach a conclusion. Politics consists of trying to make a majority of potential voters think a certain thing. The radical environmental groups in this country are telling their side of the story so often and in so many places in the hope that it will become accepted fact instead of the highly questionable proposition that it really is. In time, unless scientific inquiry is scuttled, it may turn out that there is no more to global warming caused by human activity than there was to the stories spread in the 1930s in Germany that Jewish people were responsible for the pitiful state of the German economy.

The environmental groups join the American Left, labor unions, and trial lawyers as essential supporters and puppet masters of our for-hire federal legislators. The grip held by environmental groups on the Democratic Party has prevented us from obtaining oil and natural gas that is easily available within our borders and our coastal waters. The science on which their advocacy is based is founded on hysteria and political opinion rather than real science. Oil has been explored for and extracted in the United States for about 150 years, beginning in Pennsylvania, Texas, and Oklahoma—not exactly unpopulated areas—without any significant environmental impact. Opposition to exploration and drilling in a small corner of the Arctic National Wildlife Refuge (ANWR) is political, not scientific. It arises from the same cynical, vote-buying mentality that wants to impose a special windfall profits tax on the very businesses that are using much of their profits to enhance their ability to produce oil-based energy for us. According to a United States Geological Survey published in April 2008, an area of North Dakota and Montana known as the Bakken Formation has between three and four and one-third billion barrels of recoverable oil, an amount that would make oil-producing "friends" like Saudi Arabia and declared enemies like Venezuela just two ordinary trade partners.[91] No matter: environmentalists and their kept lawmakers won't allow recovery or refining of that oil. And as this book is being completed, Pennsylvania, due to the wisdom of state politicians in both parties (one of them an *outgoing* governor), is about to benefit in jobs and tax revenues from the Marcellus shale formation, while green activists have killed similar opportunities for New York State.[92]

Political opposition to exploration and drilling off our coasts is similarly driven, with the added twist that Russian, Chinese, and Cuban enterprises are exploring and drilling for that same oil, with significantly less concern for the environment and a lot less technological means of avoiding oil spills. China, as of about 2006-2007, became the

---

91 Norm Alster, "U.S. Bakken Oil Output Soaring," *Investor's Business Daily*, February 9, 2011.

92 "A Tale of Two Shale States," *Wall Street Journal*, July 26, 2011.

world's leading polluter, as measured by industrial carbon emissions.[93] I would wager that neither it nor Cuba care about what, after all, is our environment, not theirs. Even if there were collateral environmental damage from drilling in ANWR or in our coastal waters, increasing the availability of oil to American businesses and consumers, and ceasing the transfer of our wealth to foreign enemies, is arguably more important. The Democrats have blocked these activities since 1995, not—in my opinion—because they have any sincere convictions, and certainly not based on any sound scientific grounds. They have blocked them to placate vocal environmentalists, many of whom are one-issue fanatics, in order to remain in office.

There are oil refineries within this country, but no new refinery has been built for decades. The number of refineries has declined from 324 in 1981 to 141 in 2009.[94] That is mainly because of a crushing burden of federal regulations that makes the cost of building and operating new refineries prohibitive. Senators and representatives know that new refineries are needed and that these refineries would increase our supply of gasoline and other oil products, thereby reducing their cost. They keep the regulations in place to please the environmentalists. Left-wing writers have argued that new oil refineries would not reduce the cost of gasoline. That advocacy is politically driven and mistaken. *Anything* that increases the supply of a commodity lowers the price.

Environmentalists have also succeeded in blocking the construction of any new nuclear power plants in our country for over thirty years. Nuclear power is clean and inexpensive; the fuel is readily available and will be for a long time. Since no waste is emitted, the generation of nuclear power has no effect whatsoever on the atmosphere or environment. The United States Navy has had nuclear submarines and other nuclear-powered vessels in operation since the 1950s without one accident or mishap of consequence. Such diverse nations as France, Belgium, Ukraine, Sweden, Spain, and South Korea produce between 36 percent

93 Roger Harrabin, "China 'now top carbon polluter,'" BBC News, April 14, 2008, accessed May 31, 2011, http://news.bbc.co.uk/2/ hi/734738.

94 "Talking Turki on Oil," *Investor's Business Daily*, August 27, 2009.

and 78 percent of their electricity with nuclear power plants.[95] None of these countries have reported any environmental damage because of construction or operation of nuclear plants. The problems in early 2011 at Japan's Fukushima Daiichi nuclear power plant were caused in part by the facility's proximity to a known earthquake zone. The United States, like Western Europe, is not particularly earthquake prone, and nuclear plants need not be built in San Francisco. Further, Fukushima's forty-year-old cooling system was unable to work when the power failed, a deficiency long since corrected by later nuclear technology.[96] The nuclear power plants in America, which has long been the world leader in new and better technology, produce only 19 percent of our electricity. A sufficient number of new nuclear power plants would enormously reduce our dependence on foreign or domestically produced oil. Left-wing writers argue that construction of new nuclear plants would take too long and therefore would do no good. Again, their advocacy is driven by politics, and is mistaken. The reason it takes so long to build a nuclear power plant is because politicians have imposed so many regulatory delays. Those regulations can be swept aside by the stroke of a pen.

The alleged concern of the radical environmental lobby is that if an accident ever occurred at a nuclear power plant, the environment could be damaged. Environmentalists cite an incident that occurred three decades ago, at Three Mile Island in Pennsylvania. What they and their agents in the media neglect to mention is that no one was killed or injured, no property was damaged, and there was no damage to the environment. Other than that, there have been no accidents in this country involving nuclear power. The Three Mile Island situation bears no resemblance to what happened at Chernobyl in Ukraine. There was significant damage in that case, but blame for the accident lies with inadequate Russian technology and the incompetence of those operating the plant.

95 *Energy Studies Yearbook:* 1993 (New York: United Nations 1995).

96 Rep. Dana Rohrabacher, "On the Verge of Safe Reactors that will Revolutionize World," *Investor's Business Daily*, April 1, 2011.

There is significant scientific debate about whether man-made industrial emissions are causing the temperature of the world to rise. Regardless of that issue, it is largely undisputed, except by fanatics, that major reductions in American emissions would have an infinitesimally small impact on world temperatures. American environmentalists ignore the fact that China and India are two of the world's top polluters, as well as the fact that greenhouse gas emissions from signatories to the Kyoto Treaty have increased more rapidly than ours. Instead, they press for Cap and Trade legislation. If that legislation becomes law, it will devastate American heavy industry and cause hundreds of thousands to lose their jobs. The less fanatical proponents of that law admit as much. But neither the environmentalists nor their kept politicians see the importance of China and India not agreeing to limit their emissions. Those countries, as pointed out in chapter 6, will not willingly do anything that would compromise their industrial development, which they see as in their national interest. The national interest of nations like China is the reason the environmental summit conference in early 2010 ended with no binding or enforceable limits on industrial emissions. None of that matters to the Sierra Club and other well-funded environmental groups, which think our country should unilaterally limit such emissions despite the potential job losses and loss of GDP.

In light of the serious damage to American industry that emission control could cause, we need federal legislators in office who are not obligated to environmentalists. We instead need independent thinkers who will measure the value of increased industrial production and economic strength against possible damage to the environment if industrial emission controls are not required.

Democrats have tried to obfuscate their motives by attempting to force alternative energy sources on the American public. As reported on August 13, 2010, in *Investor's Business Daily*, the Chevy Volt, an electric and gas-powered automobile built by General Motors with monstrous tax-funded subsidies, has a limited range and is too pricy to compete in the automobile market. There is very limited consumer interest in the Volt, despite the billions in bailout money and grants spent on its development.[97] That's only one example of federal lawmakers telling private citizens what they should be buying. A lot of time is also wasted talking about solar and wind power. They have their roles, but they are small roles and will stay small. In 2011 so-called green energies, including wind, solar, and biomass, produce only 3.6 percent of the fuel used to produce electricity in America, even after decades of government subsidies.[98] Spain found that 2.2 jobs were lost because of each green job created.[99] There is no hope that green energy can replace energy derived from oil, coal, natural gas, and nuclear fission anytime in the foreseeable future.

Another favorite alternative energy source of the Left is food, in the form of corn and other grains, commodities that are desperately needed for animal and human consumption around the world. Enormous quantities of corn and other grains are processed at great expense into ethanol, a fuel that produces less energy than gasoline and can harm small motors. Ethanol is mixed with gasoline in a ratio of about 10 percent ethanol to 90 percent gasoline. Its helpful environmental impact, if any, is nugatory. The negative impact of ethanol production on worldwide food supplies and prices, on the other hand, has been astronomical. Ethanol production has caused hundreds of thousands of people around the world to face deprivation and even starvation because of the high prices of food or its unavailability.[100] It also uses a disproportionate amount of water, a scarce resource in some states even now, and causes damaging soil erosion.[101]

The quickest route to relief from oil dependence and high oil prices is nuclear power. Nuclear power plants can be built around the country by the private sector much more quickly than oil can be extracted

---

97 "Keep On Truckin'," *Investor's Business Daily*, January 4, 2011.

98 "Pump and Circumstance," *Investor's Business Daily*, March 31, 2011.

99 Ibid.

100 Hans Bader, "Deadly Ethanol Subsidies Cause Famine and Hunger," Examiner.com, June 6, 2010, accessed November 24, 2010, http://www.examiner.com.

101 David Pimentel and Marcia Pimentel, "Corn and Cellulosis Ethanol Cause Major Problems," Energies 2008, June 17, 208, accessed November 24, 2010, www.mdpr.org/energies.

from ANWR, the North American coastal shelf, Rocky Mountain oil shale fields, or the Bakken Formation. Nonetheless, for reasons that are unscientific and ideological, the environmental lobby will not allow us to build nuclear plants. Nor will they allow us to do the other things that are necessary, although they will take longer.

Politicians in the Senate and House do the bidding of environmentalists on all the issues on the environmentalists' agenda. That agenda favors environmental concerns at great expense to our economy. In a November 22, 2010, article in *Investor's Business* Daily titled "The Climate Cash Cow," Ottmar Edenhofer, co-chair of the U.N. Intergovernmental Panel on Climate Change, is quoted as stating that "climate policy is redistributing the world's wealth." Our federal lawmakers have in many cases catered to that agenda, despite evidence that extreme environmental groups are part of the American Left, which advocates reducing American importance in the world and sees American economic decline as a way to make that happen. Those legislators probably have no convictions on the issue, and likely no technical knowledge. They simply do what they are told by their masters in the environmental lobby, in the same manner that they do the bidding of labor unions and trial lawyers. Democrats probably know that successful research and development of new and better products, including new sources and increased supplies of energy, come from a motivated private sector free of unnecessary government regulation. They simply don't care. Their goal is to stay in office, and to do that they think they should increase taxes on oil companies, continue the excessive and restrictive regulation of the entire energy industry, inflict the Cap and Trade law on us, and continue discouraging nuclear-generated energy, because that is what environmental activists demand. For too many of our congresspeople, remaining in power is more important than anything else, including the interests of America and its citizens. They'll worry about that later, or better yet, let someone else worry about it later. That's why they deserve only one term. Environmental groups, no more than labor unions or lawyers, should not control decisions on national policy. Our future hinges on those decisions being made by unbought legislators with no selfish career plans.

CHAPTER 11

The Plaintiffs' Trial Lawyers

Lawyers, upon admission to the bar, take an oath to uphold the law, to act ethically, and to zealously support the interests of their clients. There is nothing in the attorney's oath about making money, let alone getting rich from working as a lawyer. Many lawyers work long hours, exert great effort on behalf of their clients, and make a reasonable living. There are many lawyers who work hard to make modest livings.

The part about modest livings does not apply, however, to the most successful and thus most highly paid lawyers—those who represent plaintiffs in contingency fee litigation. They are called trial lawyers in the media, although in fact they are only one highly specialized type of litigation attorney. The attorneys discussed in this chapter are among the most competent, well-organized, and wealthy individuals in this country. The only reason they are relevant to *American Manifesto* is that their persuasive power, fueled by money, exerts great influence on elected lawmakers who want to stay elected, and thus helps determine the nature and fate of many legislative initiatives.

Let me say at this point that I do not have the same view of the men and women I discuss here as I do of the American Left, labor unions, and radical environmentalists. I am, after all, a practicing corporate attorney with substantial courtroom experience. The most successful plaintiffs' trial lawyers are, like all of us, driven by self-interest. In a modern money economy, most individuals who can do so "go where the money is." I, unlike leftist politicians and their followers, don't envy or blame well-paid achievers for their success. The trial lawyers who are germane here are, with few exceptions, ethical and fine men and women. One of the best of them is a close friend, and a more honorable man never practiced law. My concern is not with trial lawyers—it is with elected politicians whose overriding hunger for remaining in office overpowers their concern for the national interest and thus causes them to solicit and accept large amounts of the trial lawyers' money.

That said, who are these people? Literally, trial lawyers are lawyers who conduct litigation in courts. Many of them work hard, conscientiously, and skillfully for reasonable amounts of money. The trial lawyers who are important to elected politicians are an aggregation of the highest-paid lawyers that prosecute large civil cases in exchange for contingency fees. There are not that many of them, but they hold great power. The areas of law in which they operate are personal injury, medical malpractice, products liability, consumer finance, securities law, employment law, and any other that will generate enormous fees. These lawyers receive fees ranging from 25 percent to 40 percent of the settlements or recoveries they receive.

When possible, trial lawyers bring civil actions as class actions. A class action is a civil action brought on behalf of a group or a class of persons found by the trial court to have similar interests and similar claims. They are therefore entitled to proceed in unison against a defendant. Classes of plaintiffs can number in the hundreds of thousands. Class actions are typically brought against large corporate defendants with large amounts of money. Plaintiffs' lawyers know that when a trial judge certifies a civil action as a class action, the corporate defendant has little choice but to settle the case with a substantial monetary payment. Otherwise, it will bear the enormous cost and risk of defending that case through trial. Almost all class actions are settled short of trial because of the cost and monetary risk to the defendants. Plaintiffs' lawyers also know that corporate defense counsel often have little stomach for long, difficult trials, which take months to process and which place their corporate clients at risk. Corporate defense lawyers typically receive large fees (based on billing by the hour) for the early and easier stages of major litigation. They usually find reasons to advise their clients to settle out of court before they and the client have to undergo the discipline, rigor, and risk of a long trial. Plaintiffs' lawyers know that, and cash in on the knowledge.

There are many examples of settlements of class actions in which thousands of class members received small amounts of money—while the attorneys received millions. In some class actions, the relief obtained for the class consisted primarily of changes in the practices of whatever industry was being targeted, with class members receiving insignificant amounts of money. Under the law, that does not stop courts from awarding fees to the class members' attorneys.

This book is not about lawyers. The highest level of plaintiff's attorneys are relevant here because they unintentionally contribute to the difficulties faced by our country, due to the corruptibility of elected politicians. They mainly support candidates of the Democratic Party. The Democratic Party would be a less viable political party without trial lawyers. Wrote nationally syndicated Charles Krauthammer on July 26, 2009, "The Democrats are parasitically dependent on huge donations from trial lawyers." In my opinion, these highly skilled and wealthy lawyers do not help finance Democratic campaigns because of their concerns about domestic or foreign policy, although they may have such concerns. They contribute heavily because they are concerned, and rightly so, that senators and representatives will propose and pass legislation that reduces contingency fees and lowers punitive damage awards. Other laws could give potential defendants partial immunity from some civil actions for reasons of national security or make it more difficult for courts to order class certification every time a group of self-proclaimed victims contends that it has been injured by something. The plaintiffs' trial lawyers understandably want to keep things in their industry just the way they are, and they wield power over elected politicians to that end. It is fair to question whether such power has a debilitating effect on the private-sector economy, which includes health care and the health insurance industries.

It is no accident that trial lawyers heavily supported Barack Obama for president. Trial lawyers poured huge amounts of money into his campaign, and are one of the major funders of his party.[102] Nationwide, trial lawyers give enormous sums to the campaigns of Democratic senators and representatives. I do not believe this is because trial lawyers are focused on any programs, projects, or agendas that have to do with the welfare of this country or its citizens. The reason they contribute money is because they want to continue making money by suing rich defendants, primarily large corporations. It is no accident that among all the competing ideas being discussed in the debate over a government-controlled health care system, plaintiffs' lawyers and their organizations made successful efforts to exclude tort reform from the outcome. That is confirmed by the earlier cited March 26, 2010, letter from Anthony Tarricone, President of the American Association for Justice (AAJ), formerly the Association of Trial Lawyers of America (ATLA), to the members of AAJ. Tarricone wrote that he was "very pleased to report that the healthcare [sic] bill is clear of any provisions that would limit an injured patient's rights concerning medical negligence claims." He cited as highlights the AAJ's defeat of tort reform amendments in all three committees that amended the original legislation, subsequent defeat of twenty-eight other tort reform amendments, the AAJ's defeat in the Senate of a cap on attorney's fees, the AAJ's huge media campaign to "educate" lawmakers (and the public), and AAJ's purchase of "all the billboard space" in the subway station used by Senate staffers. Tarricone did not mention who paid for all of that, nor did he need to. Thus, although the entire stated reason for health care reform is cost, and despite the undisputed fact that tort litigation drives up that cost, a relatively small number of successful and wealthy lawyers helped to exclude tort reform from the bill. That was one of the largest political paybacks in American history.

102 Fred Barnes, "Caving to Trial Lawyers," *The Weekly Standard*, September 7, 2009.

I earlier cited the Foreign Intelligence Surveillance Act (FISA), which allows surveillance of communications between those in foreign countries and this country who are suspected of being terrorists. It is, of course, impossible to prove in courts of law that all of them are involved in terrorism. A government that has to defend its citizens has to be trusted to monitor communications between dangerous individuals and groups. Speaker Pelosi and her cronies allowed FISA to lapse, leaving us unprotected for months. How and why were trial lawyers involved? Large telecommunications companies have been sued in class actions by trial lawyers on behalf of left-leaning groups, including the American Civil Liberties Union. These groups claim that their rights were abused by the telecommunications companies because those companies cooperated with federal investigators. The companies asked for protective legislation so that when they allow monitoring of communications between terrorists bent on the destruction of American lives and property, they will not be sued. One would think that Pelosi and her like would have put aside partisan differences, regardless of the desires of trial lawyers. Wrong. Trial lawyers, the money they give senators and representatives, and the desire of those individuals to remain in office, helped cause the lapse of FISA. Federal legislators hate it when their loyalty is questioned, but their obedience to forces such as rich lawyers makes one wonder whose side they are on. As I see it, they were more interested in remaining in office than in ensuring that the lives and property of American citizens were protected.

Another example happened in April and May of 2008, in central Florida. Congress made three hundred million dollars available to help in the building of a commuter rail system in central Florida, one of the fastest growing areas in the country. A commuter rail system in central Florida would arguably save uncountable millions of passenger miles of automobile travel between homes and jobs, and between homes and recreation sites. At a time when the cost of gasoline was over $4.00 per gallon, the roads were crowded, and liberals were in hysterics about man- and machine-made emissions, one would think a commuter rail system would not be controversial. It isn't, except for the trial lawyers. Why is that? In order for commuter rail to happen, at least in central Florida, rail has to be bought or leased from railroad companies, primarily CSX Transportation. CSX is concerned about future litigation against it if it makes its property and track available for high-speed commuter rail. As part of the legislation, which was killed on May 2, 2008, CSX wanted certain caps and limits on its liability. The trial lawyers in Florida and their association killed the legislation. Appeals by legislators to prominent Florida trial lawyers were rebuffed. One writer in the *Orlando Sentinel* referred to the Democratic state legislators who killed that legislation as "lap dogs for trial lawyers."

There are other examples. However, in deciding on candidates in November 2012, a legitimate question is whether we want trial lawyers and their organizations to have a disproportionate role in running our government. And, more importantly, do we want senators and representatives in office who are more concerned with their tenure than with good legislation, and who are willing to tailor laws to appease trial lawyers because of the money such lawyers give them? Limiting federal legislators to one term would remove the reason for the money piñatas trial lawyers dangle, election after election, in front of candidates in order to persuade them to do their bidding.

CHAPTER 12

Federal Taxation, Fair and Unfair

This chapter begins with two questions.

If you were an elected federal legislator, and you could use the power of your office to manipulate the tax code and levy taxes to please and support those interests that keep you in office and to control, penalize, and punish groups and individuals whose interests are adverse to yours or those of your supporters, would you do those things? Answer: you would, and they do.

If you were a private citizen or a private business entity and could abolish the Internal Revenue Service and all its ancillary tax collection and enforcement mechanisms; do away with all payroll taxes, all federal income taxes on individuals and corporations, and the federal estate tax; not have to file a tax return and pay someone to prepare it; and instead pay one simple tax on all goods and services you purchased, *with the federal government receiving the same amount of money per year that it now receives from all taxes it collects,* what would be your choice? Before you decide, know that part of a yes answer would entail, for the first time, visitors to the United States, including illegal aliens, paying the same tax you pay on acquisitions of goods and services. Moreover, billions of dollars being earned by criminal activity that are now untaxed would be taxed. Even crooks, which include illegal immigrants, need to buy things. Also know that the abolition of an income tax on corporations would cause many United States and foreign corporations to do business here and employ people here, instead of abroad. Hold your answer to the second question until you finish this chapter.

The first question, which has to do with the relationship between the power of federal legislative officeholders and how federal taxation works, describes what happens today. It has been increasingly the case since the inception of what is known as the progressive income tax.

Taxes on income were unknown to the founders of the United States. A tax on income is a relatively new concept. Since the 1930s, Congress has increasingly imposed a disproportionately high tax burden on the individuals who earn the most money. For decades Congress has used taxation as an instrument of social policy, to reward favored groups and punish others. Taxation is used to maintain the class warfare between the supposed rich and the poor, with the votes of the latter being bought with money taken from the former. The current tax system gives legislators power over the people and businesses that drive our economy. The proclivity of Congress to increase tax rates and think up new sources of tax revenue is one part of the problem. The other part is Congress's addiction to spending other people's money. It has previously been discussed that members of Congress spend other people's money in large part to serve the interests of those they believe will help them remain in office. To a federal legislator, it is an irresistible win-win situation: use other people's money to stay in office, and simultaneously manipulate the tax laws so as to wield power over the most successful and productive men, women, and businesses in the country.

This chapter is not only about federal taxation. It is about how the present system of taxation is unfair and discriminatory, how unnecessarily costly and burdensome it is on American taxpayers, and how desperately federal politicians want to keep the system as is. The only legitimate purpose of a tax code and system of taxation is to raise the money necessary for the government to operate. Taxation should not be a means for anyone, regardless of political persuasion, to make social policy and regulate business activity. In this chapter, I will discuss a different system that would do at least four things. First, it would deprive Congress of the means of influencing social policy and serving the interests of their supporters, by manipulating the Internal Revenue Code; specifically, repealing the Code and replacing it with a law a million times less complex. Second, it would eliminate the truly enormous costs, inefficiency, waste, and frustration suffered by the American people in complying with the Internal Revenue Code and regulations. According to an October 21, 2011 article in *Investor's Business Daily,* complying with the Tax Code in 2011 will cost U.S. Taxpayers $431 billion. Third, it would place at the disposal of the federal government approximately the same amount of money it has received in the past. Fourth, and perhaps most important, it would remove from personal and business decision making the expensive, negative, and anti-business factor of federal taxes. Businesses would decide what is best for their customers and them without having to deal with federal tax issues. No knowledgeable and responsible American citizen should have reason to quarrel with the following proposal. However, although the concept, after many years of expensive and detailed research, has been known for thirteen years, it is bitterly opposed by most politicians, because it would deprive them of a major part of their power over us. Read that again. Those *we* elect to serve *us* have *power* over us that they will not relinquish.

Much of the subject matter of this chapter must be attributed to two people, one of whom needs no introduction to conservatives, and the other of whom is relatively unknown. The first is the radio talk show personality based in Atlanta, Neal Boortz. The other is now-retired Georgia Republican Representative John Linder. Boortz and Linder are spearheading a mass movement, which is the product of many years of research, called the FairTax. The FairTax is a consumption tax on the purchase of newly created goods and new services by anyone within the borders of the United States, citizen or otherwise. The tax is 23 percent of the stated price or cost of the new goods and services. It is not a sales tax or value added tax, both which are taxes of a certain percentage added to the price of certain goods and services. The FairTax is 23 percent of the asking price of goods and services. There is a difference. Enactment of the FairTax would result in the abolition of the Internal Revenue Service, all its employees and facilities, as well as the taxpayer-funded jobs of the tens of thousands of individuals who collect federal taxes and enforce federal tax laws, from federal judicial and courthouse employees to collection agents. Those savings alone would be astronomical. All that money could remain in the private sector. The people who lose their jobs could join the private sector and create value, instead of feeding on taxpayer money. There would be no federal individual income tax. The billions of hours of unproductive and unpaid work, and the billions of dollars spent—that is, wasted—on tax preparation and tax advice would be saved. There would be no corporate tax, meaning that corporations could do their planning and decision making, including hiring, based on legitimate business reasons, rather than on tax avoidance. There would be no federal estate tax. Under the estate tax system in place in 2011, depending on the value of the estate of a deceased business owner, many family-owned businesses would have to be sold, and their employees laid off in order to raise cash to pay the estate tax upon the death of the owner of the business. Employees working for a paycheck would know exactly how much money they were going to take home, because there would be no deductions for taxes, Social Security, or Medicare. All of those things would be paid for by the FairTax.

The nature and characteristics of the FairTax are explained in two books by Boortz and Linder, *The FairTax Book*, and the more recently published, *FairTax: The Truth*.[103] FairTax proponents claim that about one hundred and sixty million workers are paying taxes at this time through payroll taxes. Many truly wealthy people pay minimal income taxes, because while they have great wealth, they have little ordinary income that is subject to the higher ordinary income tax rates, which apply to wages and salaries. In many cases, they have capital gains,

103 Neal Boortz and John Linder, *The FairTax Book* (New York: HarperCollins Publishers, Inc. 2005); Boortz, Linder and Rob Woodall, *FairTax: The Truth* (New York: HarperCollins Publishers, Inc., 2008).

now taxed at 15 percent. That is how Warren Buffett got away with complaining that millionaires and billionaires are "coddled" by our income tax rates. In other cases wealthy people have interest income on state and municipal securities, which is nontaxable. Most of us, however, earn salaries or wages, which are taxed at the higher ordinary income rates. The FairTax proponents claim that under the FairTax about three hundred million citizens, plus another fifty million foreign visitors—some of whom are illegal—would be funding the federal treasury through their purchases. High wage-earners and the very rich would not pay Social Security and Medicare on only their first $97,500 of income, but would be taxed on *everything* they spend for new goods and services. It is estimated that the FairTax would double the revenues to Social Security, Medicare, and Medicaid in twenty years or less. Tax fraud would be impossible: if you buy a new good or service, you pay the FairTax. This alone would add tens of billions to the treasury.

The less obvious merits of the FairTax are its incalculable indirect benefits to the American economy. We have discussed the nature of economies in general, and how a strong free-market economy is the vital foundation of a strong nation. Businesses, both small and large, would no longer have to make crucial business decisions based on corporate income tax considerations, as there would be no corporate income tax. Corporations could, and would, have their headquarters in the United States, and would draw their workers from the American workforce. Doing those things would no longer incur the penalties now imposed by the United States corporate income tax, at this time the world's highest. It is a safe assertion that virtually everyone who has read Boortz and Linder's books has become an enthusiastic proponent of the FairTax. Interestingly, the major media have been silent on the subject.

So, why don't we undertake this and make it happen? As stated in *FairTax: The Truth*, the answer to that is "power." State the authors, "The more politicians can control your access to your own wealth and earnings, the more powerful they are. The more politicians can affect businesses and important business decisions with tax policy, the more powerful they are. The more they can adversely affect the financial picture of one segment of our economy for the benefit of another, the more powerful they are."[104] Boortz and Linder state elsewhere that "passing the FairTax would constitute the biggest transfer of power from government to the people in the history of this republic. In case you haven't noticed it, some politicians aren't all that fond of transferring power."[105] Boortz and Linder make no distinctions between Democrats and Republicans (Boortz is a Libertarian). They understand, as do I, that no elected politicians, unless forced to do so, will give up the power they possess. That includes the American tax code and the unforeseen, unjustified, and downright arbitrary uses to which it is being put. Senators, representatives, and the Left have erected many arguments opposing the FairTax, all of which topple when met with empirical, fact-based responses. Their only genuine argument is: "What! Give up our power to control American industry and American citizens, relinquish our ability to punish our enemies, and do without the means of rewarding those who keep us in office? Are you crazy?"

The only thing missing from the FairTax books is the point I am making here. That is that removing the ability of elected federal politicians to succeed themselves would go a long way toward giving the FairTax (and other proposals, such as the flat tax) a fair debate and an up or down vote. It seems reasonable that congresspeople in all political parties who are unconcerned with reelection would have to give the FairTax full and fair consideration. If federal politicians were not concerned with reelection, they would be more inclined to focus on the fact that the current system of taxation constitutes a serious burden on those who work hard and achieve. Almost half of working Americans pay no income taxes. The American people are entitled to an honest judgment from federal legislators on whether that is a good thing for America, or whether everyone should pay something, except for those below a poverty level. The FairTax would even benefit federal legislators because, upon their return to private life, they would have

104 Boortz and Linder, *FairTax: The Truth*, 216.

105 Ibid.,_60.

to resume earning their livings in the private sector. The FairTax is one of the most obvious issues that would receive exposure, a fair debate, and an up or down vote from federal politicians unconcerned with tenure and maintaining their power over us. The opportunity of having disinterested politicians vote on this compelling idea is one more reason why federal elected politicians should have one term only.

Now, what is your answer to the second question? Would you like to not have to deal with the IRS, and not waste millions of hours and billions of dollars on tax planning and tax compliance? Would you like to see foreign visitors, as well as illegal immigrants and other criminals, help to reduce the deficit? Would you like to reduce the power of politicians, and still adequately fund government? Would you like to have the offshore workforces of major American companies work in the United States? If so, vote:

☑ Yes ☐ No

CHAPTER 13

What Health Care Crisis?

The health care "crisis," over which federal legislators and other politicians are so worked up, is the result of at least three unnecessary factors. The first is the involvement of the federal government. Jefferson, Adams, Hamilton, and Madison would be shocked to see the federal government regulating and controlling relationships between patients, physicians, hospitals, and pharmaceuticals. A fundamental principle of American law has long been that the health and welfare of the people is a matter of what is called the "police power" of states; that is, the power to protect the health and welfare of citizens of states. Federal Intervention in patient care and patient choices is a relatively new and highly controversial proposition. In the first Clinton term, Americans resoundingly shot down Hillary Clinton's plan for a national health-care system, more accurately called socialized medicine. It went down for the same reasons as did the Harriet Miers nomination and the 2007 immigration bill: it was seen as a really bad idea, we had time to learn about it and understand it, and we did not want it. The Clintons, unlike the Obama administration and its minions in Congress, made it possible for us to learn what "HillaryCare" would involve by allowing us to be informed. Thus enabled, we decided not to make it happen.

In stark contrast, a small majority of lawmakers has, at least for now, forced mandatory federally controlled health care on us. The

Patient Protection and Affordable Care Act was signed on March 23, 2010 after an intense and unprecedented campaign of persuasion and propaganda, as well as promises and representations of alleged fact which many found and are finding questionable. The bill is so long and complicated that I question whether those who championed it read it. Speaker Pelosi stated publicly that "we" would need to enact the law to find out what is in it![106] It was passed in the House by a slim margin, and passed in the Senate by a procedural move, which avoided the filibuster. Senators and House members were subjected to a barrage of coercion and a smorgasbord of bribery that would be criminal in the business world. More importantly, it was passed in the face of overwhelming evidence that a majority of Americans emphatically did not want the legislation passed. The media have ignored the fact that that majority of citizens probably consisted of people who were somewhat informed on the subject. Had more been informed, as in the case of the Clintons' health-care plan, more would have opposed it. Opposition has grown since passage,[107] despite an unprecedented government public relations campaign (paid for by us) to popularize this unpopular legislation. Government control of our health care is a long-held goal of the Left. Passage of Obamacare by a tiny majority of lawmakers was a prime example of how our federal legislators do the bidding of the Left and party bosses without regard to our interests, let alone the Constitution. The overarching arrogance of federal lawmakers and their ruling-class mentality was transparently demonstrated by Speaker Pelosi who, when asked what provision of the Constitution allows the federal government to force citizens to buy a product or service, replied: "Are you kidding? Are you kidding?"[108]

A second factor in the alleged crisis, one that is independent of government interference, was based on commercial greed—the

106 David Freddoso, "Pelosi on health care: 'We have to pass the bill so you can find out what is in it . . .'," Washingtonexaminer.com, March 9, 2010, *http://washingtonexaminer.com/blogs/beltway-confidential/Pelosi-health-care-039we-have-pass-bill-so-you-can-find-out-what-it039.*, accessed September 22, 2011.

107 "The Case Builds vs. ObamaCare," *Investor's Business Daily*, June 9, 2011.

108 Codevilla, *The Ruling Class*, 45.

unnecessary, unwanted, and costly intrusion of the non-medically trained business community into our health-care system. This intrusion is euphemistically called managed care. The correct name is "inefficient and unnecessarily costly interference of ignoramuses with medicine." It took the place of true health insurance, although politicians buying votes still call it insurance, because promises of "health insurance for all" sound better than promises of "managed care for all." Why did we need executives and middle managers who don't know a wart from a mole taking money from us, money that would otherwise go on a supply-and-demand basis to direct providers of diagnoses, treatment, surgery, hospitalization, and medicines? And who needs clerical staff telling our physicians what tests to run and how many days of hospitalization are required?

Politicians and businesspeople trying to sell the public on managed care and socialized medicine claim that physicians are greedy and must be forced to keep their fees down. Not only does that contravene the laws of supply and demand—if the practice of medicine becomes overly lucrative, more people will become physicians and drive down the cost—but it is otherwise a highly dubious claim. Anyone who has ever had a relationship with an American medical college and American medical students is aware of the high quality of the education and training, as well as the dedication and selflessness, of the faculties and students. It is pitiful that medical doctors, unlike lawyers, have allowed themselves to be regulated and controlled by garden-variety businesspeople who, much like labor unions, are being paid a lot of money for an unnecessary service. This has happened, in all likelihood, for the same reasons that many medical doctors, as intelligent as they have to be to successfully study medicine, are notoriously poor at handling their financial affairs. The ultimate consequence of managed care and national health care may be a serious decline in the number of bright young Americans willing to be physicians.

The third major factor in the problems of health care is the lucrative system of tort litigation practiced by trial lawyers against physicians, hospitals, health insurers, and drug manufacturers. Although tort litigation has been with us since the founding of our country, medical malpractice litigation is a fairly new thing. Gigantic awards handed out by juries are even newer. In large medical malpractice cases, paid medical experts on both sides offer opinions on whether the diagnosis or treatment in question met the requisite standard of care. In many cases, one or both experts are being paid big money to exaggerate or lie. A jury of individuals who know nothing about medicine decides whether the standard was met or not met, and how much money to award the plaintiff. Plaintiffs' lawyers typically take 33.3 percent to 40 percent of the recovery, after being reimbursed for their expenses. This is a huge financial drain on the entire health-care industry. It also causes doctors to perform unnecessary tests in order to avoid potential litigation, thereby driving up their fees and expenses. While tort reform should be a matter for states to deal with, the fact that the United States Senate and House of Representatives steadfastly refused to even consider tort reform in passing Obamacare is a stark reminder of how much influence trial lawyers and their organizations have. The various proposals for a national health-care system that received serious consideration by Congress had one common feature: the complete absence of any medical malpractice litigation reform. Decisions on this matter should not be left to politicians who are under the control of plaintiffs' trial lawyers.

The Senate and House were not responsible for managed care. But laws they could easily change make it hard for physicians and other health-care providers to band together and drive the businesspeople and money managers out of the picture. At the least, Congress could allow us to buy health plans nationwide, as opposed to the current requirement of having to shop in-state. Congress could also greatly improve the efficiency and response time of pharmaceutical companies by just getting out of the way. However, it's just too politically beneficial to call it the "drug industry" and regulate it half to death, in an effort to make voters think incumbent legislators care about them and are doing something about a problem they helped create.

If national health care remains in effect, and if care deteriorates and the economy suffers, the blame will lie squarely on our senators and representatives. The federal legislators who are in favor of socialized medicine for us will always have their own superior health care. They will not be in a position in which federal employees can decide when and whether they receive life-saving treatment. But there are votes to be bought, and they think a majority of voters will ultimately buy the idea of openly and directly taxing the wealthy, and clandestinely taxing the rest of us, to pay for what they are trying to sell to us—supposedly better and less costly healthy care for all—even to the many who don't need or want it.

Socialized medicine has been an overall failure wherever it has been imposed. Both wealthy people and desperate people in Britain, Canada, and other nations that have state-operated medical care flock to other countries where they can pay cash for prompt, responsive, and competent medical care. In countries with socialized medicine, care and treatment are rationed and delayed. If Ted Kennedy had been under the plan he so breezily advocated for the masses, he would have died long before he did.

To fathom what Obamacare will cost, know that in 1968, total federal spending was $178.1 billion. In 2007, it had risen to $2,728.9 billion, meaning that the United States budget increased 15.3 times in forty years. However, spending for Social Security rose from $23.3 billion in 1968 to $581.4 billion in 2007, an increase of twenty-five times. Medicare rose from $5.1 billion in 1968 to $436 billion in 2007, an increase of 85.5 times over forty years.[109] Does anyone really think Obamacare will not increase spending in the same fashion?

An issue to consider is whether the extreme and aggressive push for Obamacare was even based on the merits of government-run health care, or instead on leftist ideology that favors increased government control of citizens' private affairs. No administration in history, no Speaker of the House, and no Senate Majority Leader have ever fought

109 Rudy Boschwitz and Tim Penny, former United States Senator and Representative respectively from Minnesota, "Government-Run Care Is a Study in Soaring Costs," *The Politics of Health Care*, July 30, 2009.

with such force and aggression to impose a peacetime measure on a highly skeptical and increasingly unwilling American public. Never has a federal government ridiculed, marginalized, and depicted as enemies groups and persons who oppose its ideas. Never has an administration bribed so many legislators in order to obtain their votes. Such conduct on the part of business executives would result in indictments and convictions. And why, after passage, is the government flogging the legislation around the country, trying in vain to make us like it?

A key point is that Obamacare is not insurance reform. The concept of insurance involves an insurer being paid money to assume risks that it contracts to assume. The risks to be insured against and the costs of the insurance (premiums) are a matter of free-market bargaining, based on what consumers need or think they need, and what it will cost the insurer to assume the selected risks, In the case of health insurance, that would include present and projected future health conditions. Due to competition, some insurers are willing to assume more and greater risks at less cost than others. It is a lie to call Obamacare insurance reform. In fact, it is welfare. Under it, insurers are forced to cover pre-existing conditions and other costly risks, and are regulated as to how much they can charge. Taxpayers pay the excess costs. Arguments that Obamacare will do away with private health insurance *and* will greatly exceed the government's cost estimates were met with a combination of lies, distortions, and vagueness, flavored with a high level of anger toward the opposition.

Whether federal spending on Obamacare will increase beyond the estimates propounded by its supporters, and whether it should be repealed, cannot and need not be decided now. After all, this book is not intended to advocate positions. It instead urges that disinterested elected politicians should conscientiously decide all of the important questions discussed herein on their merits, instead of by being dictated to, lied to, and bullied by Pelosi, Reid, and other elected politicos.

Socialized medicine, which politicians are calling "affordable health care for all, funded by higher taxes on the rich," looks a lot like another one of the politicians' vote-buying programs. It also means federal control over an intimate part of the private lives of American citizens. Nonetheless, the legislators who hyped and pushed Obamacare so hard do not need to be concerned with whether it's a good or bad idea. Why should they? They will still have their own excellent health-care system. All I ask is to have all these vital decisions made on the actual merits, by congresspeople who have no motive to buy votes and successive terms.

CHAPTER 14

Social Security

Except in the minds of many members of Congress, the consensus about Social Security is that it is bankrupt. Even that, however, is inaccurate. Bankruptcy is a legal status from which an organization is supposed to regroup and recover. For our Social Security system, if it continues in its present form, there will be no recovery. In a few years, there simply will be no money to pay to individuals who retire and qualify for benefits. The trustees of the so-called Social Security trust fund reported in May 2011 that the fund would be empty in 2036.[110] The money that was collected to pay benefits has been taken by Congress and spent on other things. As stated by Charles Krauthammer in a column entitled "Much Ado about an Empty Lockbox," which appeared in the *Orlando Sentinel* on March 20, 2011, President Obama's budget chief, Jack Lew, "acknowledges that the Social Security surpluses of the last decade were siphoned off to the Treasury Department and spent." Any like act in the private sector would be a serious criminal offense. Bernard Madoff is serving 150 years for similar conduct. In July 2011, President Obama admitted, in so many words, that the decades of government promises about the Social Security "Trust Fund" and benefits being

110 Jed Graham, "Social Security and Medicare Finances Continue to Falter," *Investor's Business Daily*, May 16, 2011.

"guaranteed" was a long-playing lie.[111] The money on hand and the money being collected are not adequate to pay the promised benefits to the mass of individuals who will soon be retiring.

Contributing to this is that, in the coming years there will be dramatically fewer individuals working and paying into Social Security, relative to the increasing number of individuals who will not be working and will be expecting benefits. In 1940 there were 160 workers for every retiree receiving social security payments, in 1950 there were 16.5, and today there are only three![112] The payroll tax levied on the paychecks of the American working class, so courted by politicians, is an increasingly large part of federal taxation. Much of that money goes to prop up Social Security. At some time in the near future, those who are working will predictably not tolerate being taxed to pay monthly stipends to idle people, most of whom could still work in some capacity if they were willing. A terrible reckoning is coming unless major measures are taken.

What can be done about this? The solution is simple and harsh, requires some advance explanation, and will not be undertaken by the present crop of career-minded federal legislators.

The Constitution contains no right of individuals to cease working and have their expenses, even some of them, paid by money earned by someone else. The founders of this country did not contemplate a system whereby people who worked would be taxed in order to support those not working. Social Security was one of many government programs developed by the supposed geniuses Franklin Roosevelt gathered during his first term, called the "brain trust." This group is also responsible for forcing employers to accept union organization of their employees, and to pay wages not determined by the free market. Like other New Deal programs, Social Security had some initial appeal and some arguable early validity, but has now gone haywire due to the abusive conduct of federal lawmakers.

---

111 "Giving Lie to the 'Lockbox,'" *Investor's Business Daily*, July 14, 2011.

112 Charles Krauthammer, "Ponzi would've made ideal Social Security Commissioner," *Orlando Sentinel*, September 18, 2011.

When Social Security was first proposed, there were two things in this country which no longer exist. One was a much lower life expectancy. In 1900, the average life expectancy was 47 years. By 1932, it was 62 years. Now it is almost 80 years.[113] Second, in 1932, we still had the same work ethic that carried this country to industrial and economic supremacy. Men who were able to work did so, earned money, and either spent it on their families or saved and invested it. Some women worked, but primarily they took care of their families. The work ethic of American women was a factor in our winning World War II. In 1932, the notion of millions of people living in full or in part at the government's expense was unheard of. No one but a 1960s radical or a committed leftist can seriously argue that the country in 1932 did not have a better work ethic than now, and a culture that featured more self-reliance and accountability. According to Dr. Krauthammer, "Social Security was not meant to provide two decades of greens fees for baby boomers."[114]

Today, huge numbers of men and women who could work, don't want to work at all. They prefer that the government take care of them. Enormous numbers of unmarried young men and women of all races are bearing child after child that will have to be supported by the government or starve. Coupled with that is the fact that when workers reach their mid-60s, they expect to be paid by the government for the rest of their lives by means of Social Security.

I am not smart enough to recommend everything that should be done about the poor; or the nonexistent work ethic and the lack of skills among many people, young and old; and the proclivity of unskilled and impoverished young people to have multiple babies out of wedlock that they cannot support. However, the easy solution to Social Security, other than the abolition of it, is pretty obvious. The solution is to substantially raise the age at which able-bodied men and women are eligible to receive free money from the labors of others. There is no good reason for an able-bodied man or woman to retire as

113 Ibid.

114 Ibid.

early as age sixty-two, and have others pay part or all of his or her living expenses. The retirement age for healthy men and women should be raised to at least sixty-nine, and probably seventy. *That should be done now, not many years into the future; and not by slow increments, but all at once.* People who have worked at stressful careers might decide before that age to switch to something less taxing, but there is no reason why enormous numbers of people who are now retired and idle should not be earning a living doing something.

Where will all the jobs come from? Allow an unbought Congress to enact the FairTax and start counting.

My companion recommendation on this is, of course, that people who are physically unable to work should qualify for Social Security disability benefits. At this time, due to the ineptitude that is characteristic of the government, it takes years to qualify for Social Security disability benefits. That is very difficult for individuals who cannot work at all. It is wrong, and would be easy to change.

It would be of great benefit to the American economy for older Americans with good health and usable skills to be contributing to the economy instead of being a drain on it. There is no valid reason for such people to be idle and dependent on an already beleaguered workforce.

How will this happen? There is not a prayer of it happening, unless we enact one-term limits. The American Association of Retired People and legions of people younger than I will take great offense at this recommendation. They will aggressively support federal legislators who promise to "leave your Social Security alone." Remember Al Gore's 2000 mantra about placing Social Security taxes in a "lockbox"? That was a lie, because during Gore's time in the Senate and as vice president, the Ponzi-like misappropriation of Social Security monies by Congress was well underway. Florida United States Senator Marco Rubio risked his chances of being elected by talking honestly about the future of Social Security in a 2010 debate with Florida Governor Charlie Crist, who offered only the usual meaningless platitudes about waste, fraud, and abuse. Rubio then placed his seat in the upper chamber at risk in early 2011 by proposing meaningful social Security reform. Raising the retirement age won't resonate with senior citizens or Congress. Many of the former, having paid into the system, expect to be paid to be idle; and all of the latter like to control our money, because that is how they increase their power over us. Few, if any, senior citizens understand that the alternative to my proposal may be a government-controlled system that will weed out—that is, allow to die—the older, weaker, and less affluent of them. Raising the retirement age for able-bodied seniors will have to be forced on them, after full and transparent debate. Who can forget the destructive anger of mobs in France in 2010, railing and raging against a modest increase in a very young retirement age? But raising the age will save Social Security and can save our economy from disaster. The only politicians who will enact it are legislators who, serving their only term, cannot be reelected and therefore do not care about being reelected. They will know they have no choice but to do the difficult but necessary thing for their country.

This book purposely does not deal with the even more financially threatening subject of Medicare. Although its costs are even more out of control than those of Social Security, the solutions are more complicated than the easy solution suggested herein for Social Security. Raising the eligibility age would help, but other changes also seem necessary. Medicare is just as likely, if not more so, to destroy the United States' economy if federal legislators continue to have reelection as an option, because lawmakers who deal realistically and effectively with Medicare would be foregoing a further term.

CHAPTER 15

Pressure from Both Sides

Selfish, single-issue extremism is driven by ideology and money, but not necessarily any one ideology. Lest anyone think pressure that skews legislative decision making comes only from the Left, let us examine two right-wing groups that for years have exerted considerable pressure on senators and representatives. The same principles discussed above about legislative decisions being made by unduly influenced legislators apply to pressure and influence applied from the Right.

The National Rifle Association (NRA) is about as right-wing a group as exists. Its funding for its favorite candidates is less than put into play by labor unions and trial lawyers, but it is still considerable. The NRA can correctly be called a one-issue group, concerned with its agenda of promoting gun ownership to the virtual exclusion of the other important (many would say more important) issues facing our country.

The NRA, like labor unions, has been with us for many decades. Like leftist organizations, it is not adverse to masking its real agenda. The NRA sells itself as an organization that promotes the use of sporting weapons for hunters and target shooters. That is only partly true. The true overall goal of the NRA appears to be having one or more firearms in every home, with little or no restrictions on what kind. The NRA aggressively and expensively fights every attempt by legislators, state or federal, to impose any sort of regulation on firearm ownership and usage. One likely result of the NRA's rigid stance on fully automatic firearms, also called assault weapons, is the widespread use of such American-made weapons by the Mexican drug cartels. One ridiculous extreme promoted by the gun lobby is the ownership of such weapons by individuals. The NRA's cover story is that such weapons are suitable for hunting. That is poppycock. There is no reason for private individuals to own the sort of automatic weapons used by armed forces around the world. No wild animals have ever threatened hunters with a military operation. Aside from Jimmy Carter's renowned aquatic attack rabbit, they just want to be left alone.

Another initiative of the NRA of questionable value is a recently passed law in Florida which bars physicians from asking patients, including those with small children, whether they have firearms in their homes.[115] The law, placed on hold by a court ruling, originally provided for jail time for miscreant physicians![116]

The NRA is a major factor before and during every meeting of virtually every legislature, notably including the United States Congress. The one-term limit proposed in this book is not needed just to prevent senators and representatives from supporting leftist causes in order to gain additional terms. The same principle applies to the undue persuasion which the NRA, and organizations like it, are able to level at federal legislators because of the latter's desire to remain in office.

There are many other right-wing groups worth mentioning, but the extreme right-to-life groups are as good as any, and better than most. There are voters to whom the "right to life" is their only electoral issue, and there are federal politicians who will tell them what they want to hear. They are a prime reminder that it is not only the Left that insists on minding other peoples' business. Legislation on whether women should be allowed to abort unborn children should, in my opinion, be for the states to implement, since it implicates the crime of homicide,

115 Aaron Deslatte, "'Docs vs. Glocks': Judge blocks law on gun questions," *Orlando Sentinel*, September 15, 2011.

116 Ibid.

and should not be part of federal political campaigning. It seems little more than common knowledge and common sense that an abortion does constitute the intentional termination of a human life, or a soon-to-be human life. Abortion is therefore well within the police power of states to deal with; and in a more perfect country it would not be a subject of debate in congressional elections or any other federal arena. Federal legislators should not be led by reelection desires to fabricate positions on this highly personal, even spiritual, issue to placate what I see as conservative extremists.

The reason abortion and its prevention has become a topic of discussion in the federal setting is because the Senate has the right to advise and consent the appointment of all federal judges, including Supreme Court justices. The federal judiciary, rightly or wrongly, has taken over the role of elected state lawmakers in dealing with abortion issues. It is a matter of record that Senator Obama voted against the confirmation of Justices Roberts and Alito primarily because he believed that the court, with more Republican appointees, would overturn Roe v. Wade. Roe is the nearly forty-year-old case that established certain guidelines under which abortions can be legally performed, regardless of state law. Conservatives claim, with some legal basis, that the court majority in Roe fabricated a right of privacy that does not exist in the Constitution.

Leaving aside the merits of that discussion, the relevant point is that United States senators should be evaluating federal judges on their merits as legal scholars and as honest, conscientious men and women. Instead, they are susceptible to persuasion and outright coercion from groups who believe that no pregnancy should ever be terminated under any circumstances for any reason; and from groups which claim that unborn babies are fungible commodities that can be weeded out for any reason. Again, aside from the correctness or incorrectness of either position, senators will continue to be subject to undue pressure on the abortion issue, and they may skew their decisions in favor of whichever fiction they think will keep them in office.

The most recent example of successful pressure on federal lawmakers by conservative forces began in January 2011. Having been a major factor in the new Republican majority in the House after the November 2010 elections, conservative activists are behind the House initiative to repeal Obamacare. The repeal did not include any measure designed to achieve an affirmative result, such as, for example, a provision to allow health insurance to be sold without regard to state borders. It is, in my view, a hastily and ill-conceived measure that has no purpose other than to placate and reward conservative activists and to maintain their electoral support. Government control of our health care system is one of the most critical subjects we face. If the Patient Protection and Affordable Care Act of 2010 is to be repealed, that needs to be done in a reasoned and rational way, with due time for study and explanation, and not in the same way as it was passed. Based, however, on what we have seen so far, conservative lawmakers behave the same as left-leaning ones, as far as their determination to remain in power is concerned.

Human nature being what it is, and the desires of elected politicians to remain in office being always paramount in their minds, the only solution is the one-term limit.

CHAPTER 16

The Only Solution

As this is written, the United States of America is in a self-inflicted decline. If the decline is not reversed, it will, in my opinion, put an end to our prosperity and place our security and sovereignty in jeopardy. In an editorial entitled "Watching America's Decline and Fall" in the December 2010 issue of *U.S. News & World Report*, Mortimer B. Zuckerman, the editor in chief, wrote that "there is a burgeoning consensus that we are witnessing an inevitable rise of the East and a decline of the West," and that the "prognosis for America is especially discouraging." Zuckerman attributes our problems largely to self-indulgent reliance on excessive government spending and a consequent unsustainable ratio of federal debt to gross domestic product. All of that is under the control of our federal lawmakers. Thus, our direction, destiny and potential economic collapse or prosperity are in the self-serving hands of those we elect to the Senate and House. As is with all humans, their first allegiance is to themselves. The American Left, the labor unions, the trial lawyers, the environmentalists, and all other groups with money and power know this, because they are laser-focused on their own interests. They, even more than members of the Senate and House, are more concerned with their own immediate interests than with the long-term prosperity, security, and overall well-being of their country. To them, somebody else can take care of the more important and difficult stuff later. Their foremost concern is their own wealth, power, and self-advancement. To those selfish ends, they avail themselves of the self-serving ambition of many of our elected federal politicians. The interests and agendas of most of the groups that exert control over our federal lawmakers are masked but identifiable. The Left has its own deliberately obscured agenda, which does not place the interests of the United States above those of other nations. It appears unconcerned about the impending financial catastrophe discussed in chapter 2.

The situation, in my opinion, is even more critical on the international front than in domestic matters. As earlier discussed, China and Russia are arming themselves at a furious pace, while we, at Russia's urging, disarm and forego implementing purely defensive antimissile systems. North Korea is fully armed despite starving its people to accomplish that. Iran is moving inexorably toward having nuclear weapons and the means to deliver them, while the United States fantasizes that talk and economic sanctions will deter it. Perhaps our leadership believes that, in an emergency, American excellence, ingenuity, self-sacrifice, and bravery will re-emerge and save us from powerful foreign antagonists. Apart from the enormous and avoidable cost in lives and money of fighting another major war, it is predictable that we would not, as we were in 1942, be granted the necessary time. As Herman Wouk pointed out through a fictional Axis general in *War and Remembrance*, the Second World War was lost by Japan in five minutes at the Battle of Midway. "The five-minute overturn that struck the Japanese nation at Midway compels a final reflection. Industrial-scientific developments since that time have made possible Midway-style lightning holocausts of entire countries."[117] In my opinion, that describes the potential fate of the United States at the hands of a ruthless enemy armed with nuclear warheads and a means of delivery.

While my own opinions about how to ensure the future of America are not obscured, I hope this book will not be taken as another appeal

117 Wouk, *War and Remembrance*, 1:357.

for readers to support a conservative agenda. Anyone who finishes this book has the ability to decide those issues without persuasion. This book is a plea that we, the American people, take the necessary action, so that the issues I discuss here, as well as others, can be decided by elected men and women who will never consider themselves an elite ruling class. The one-term limit I advocate would produce lawmakers who would make decisions based on their own independent judgment. Instead of what we now have, they would be men and women who are not, and will never be, for sale, hire, or rent.

While the necessary remedial action might consist of piecemeal changes in the laws of different states, such changes to date have been ineffective. They have only limited the number of terms the politicians can serve, and therefore have not removed reelection from the equation. They also have been subject to legal challenges on the grounds that they contradict the Constitution. The one-term limit will require an amendment to the Constitution. Self-interested federal legislators and their allies in the legal profession would not be able to find a malleable, activist judge to overturn that.

Our senators and representatives have the right and power to make a continuing series of decisions that would bring about and perpetuate prosperity at home; secure our country's position as a military power that cannot be subjected to abuse or deprivation by aggressive hostile nations or non-governmental forces like al-Qaeda; and maintain our role as the one powerful nation in the history of civilization that uses military force to free people, not conquer them. The same elected officials have it within their power to impoverish us and end America's tenure as a wealthy, self-reliant, free, and secure nation. They currently seem to be moving in the latter direction. The major legislative and presidential initiatives since January 2009, whether accomplished or still on the table, are all matters either opposed by a majority of informed citizens, passed by small majorities, or forced on us by executive fiat. The latter include orders that require compulsory union representation or union-dictated wages and benefits on projects receiving federal funding. Other examples are: government-controlled health care (opposed by a citizen majority, passed by bribery and coercion); Cap and Trade (passed in the House by bribery, coercion, and a tiny majority, and overwhelmingly feared and opposed by an informed public); the Employee Free Choice Act (opposed by all but labor unions, still being pushed by the Left); the unilateral disclosure of our nuclear weaponry, the cessation of maintenance of the same, a one-sided disarmament treaty, the near-abandonment of our missile defenses (some requested by and all approved by Russia with no known reciprocation, and implemented by presidential order with no prior public discussion); and bailouts and TARP (rushed to passage amidst public condemnation of the opposition). In my emphatic opinion, all this was done not because senators and House members took the time or made any effort to determine what would be best for America, but because party bosses, the president, labor unions, environmentalists, and other wealthy interest groups required them to do it. The president could not have rendered his executive orders, which jeopardize our security, without knowing he had support in both houses.

Thus, with our history having moved from the desperate times of the American Revolution to the seemingly safe and, for the moment, relatively prosperous times of today, the condition that lies between our federal legislators and the highest and best interest of America is their self-interest. It afflicts them and us, not because they are bad people, but because they are human. The only way all of our senators and representatives will consistently use independent and selfless judgment in legislation is if we remove temptation. That requires removal of their opportunity to run for reelection. That removal will, in turn, end the power of *all* selfish, powerful, and wealthy interests—leftist, conservative, honest or dishonest—over the members of Congress. All interest groups will remain free to express their opinions. But their opinions will no longer be coupled with the power to drive legislative decisions. It will similarly make it impossible for party bosses to coerce or bribe senators and House members to obey their wishes (to the extent that party bosses who are serving only one term themselves will have any influence-corrupted wishes). Granted, there will be many top quality, highly successful men and women, from scholars to heart surgeons to entrepreneurs, who will be limited to one four-year term, but there can be no exceptions. Happily, there are vast numbers of such people, and this one measure would ensure a continuous procession of them seeking to serve. It will also largely exclude the incompetents, as well as those who might be prone to being corrupted while in office.

My hope is that we will amend our Constitution as recommended herein and that the result will be that the best, brightest, most energetic, and most honest men and women will line up every two years and compete for one four-year term in either the House or the Senate. Then we can confidently expect them to be and do their best, unaffected by monied groups promoting their private agendas and uncontrolled by party bosses. As a result, we are likely to survive, succeed, and prosper. And because of who we are and have been since our inception as a nation, the world will be a better place.

May God save our United States of America, and bless all of you who were so generous with your effort and time in reading this book.